HEVAL

A DIARY FROM THE WAR AGAINST THE ISLAMIC STATE

Heval
A Diary from the War against Islamic State
Jorgen Nicolai
© Jorgen Nicolai 2015
All rights reserved
First edition, second printing 2015

This book is based on real events

To protect the identity of certain individuals, their names have been changed

VIDEOS AND MORE PHOTOS IN COLOR CAN ALSO BE SEEN ON THE FACEBOOK PAGE JORGEN NICOLAI
https://www.facebook.com/pages/jorgen-nicolai/357681094426296

With deep appreciation and special thanks to
all who fight against IS,
and to my Kurdish brothers and sisters, Biji Kurdistan

Lisbeth and Dale Doré
for excellent translation

Morten G. and Klaus Pedersen
for image editing and cover design

Not least, my grateful thanks to all those Facebook readers who have commented upon, and who have supported and encouraged me to publish this book

Content

1. THE DEAD DAESH 10
2. YANA AND ANAS 30
3. ASAYISH: THE SECRET POLICE 41
4. THE ROAD TO SULYMANIYAH 66
5. SAFE HOUSE 77
6. THE GUERRILLA CAMP 96
7. TIGRIS 120
8. HQ 130
9. THE ACADEMY 137
10. SEREKANI 159
11. THE WESTERN FRONT 165
12. RETURN TO THE FRONT 198
13. THE BATTLE OF TEL HAMEES 214
14. THE HUNT FOR DAESH 233
15. KEMAL 250
16. ATTACK 263
17. BACK TO THE PRESENT 278
18. THE RIVER 300

For our brothers and sisters who perished
in the battle

SEHID NAMIRIN

PREFACE

Out of the ashes of the Iraq war, an evil of unprecedented cruelty emerged. With genocide, beheadings, the crucifixion of children, rape, and the selling of young girls as sex slaves, Islamic State spread its terror across the Middle East. It had defeated and slain its enemies with ruthless efficiency. They seemed invincible.

But in the north there lives a people called the Kurds. Theirs is a culture that has existed for millennia in Anatolia, Mesopotamia and Persia. They are a persecuted people who have survived decades of repression by brutal regimes. Kurds have learned to fight for their survival. They were the only ones with the heart and determination to stand up and fight against Islamic State, also known as the Daesh.

"You shall not pass!" was their rallying cry as their land was invaded by IS. The war had reached a turning point.

1. The Dead Daesh

I couldn't see clearly what they were doing, but there were several people down there. When I heard groaning coming from the trench, I assumed that a number of them had been wounded. Our armoured vehicle would now be used for its other purpose: as a frontline ambulance. Sure enough, the wounded *hevals* (comrades) were brought in through the hatches at the back of the armoured vehicle.

The driver revved up, and we sped off in an easterly direction towards our advanced base. The driver raced and swerved, as much to avoid buildings and electricity pylons as to avoid enemy fire. Being built mostly of metal, riding inside an armoured vehicle is hardly a joyride. Unless you hold on tight, it is easy to end up being buckled and bruised.

Suddenly I heard the sound of a rocket ... *SSSHHHsss*. A RPG flew close by our armoured vehicle. Too close. **Heval** Shingal had seen where the rocket had come from, and returned fire with our own RPG. There was a massive explosion as the rocket, which Shingal had fired, hit the building behind us. Whenever Shingal fired an RPG, it left behind a huge cloud of smoke and a foul smell. You could taste the chemicals from the RPG in your mouth. If you were to stand less than a few meters behind the rocket when it was fired, you would be killed on the spot. It was therefore always challenging for Shingal to fire the RPG through the hatches of the vehicle without harming our own men. But he had long experience, especially from his many battles in Shingal town. He was one of our best RPG-shooters.

On our return to our advance base, we carried out the wounded and took a short break. I used the opportunity to take a slug of water and eat one of the rich chocolate cakes that I carried in my bag. I would always make sure I could find them easily in the supply truck, and so replenish my energy quickly before going into action again.

I could feel that the other members of our crew were none too keen about having to go back into the firing line. It was far too dangerous to look forward to driving back into hell. Yet there was part of me that looked forward to attacking the Daesh again. We were, after all, on the verge of winning the battle. I always tried to keep all my senses open, not least my sense of intuition. Our subconscious often has a better 'feel' than the logical part of our brains. I understood that it was this kind of combativeness that would, sooner or later, lead to my downfall – if I submitted to it too often.

But we now had infantry in the city, and we had to support them.

Although we had the protection of the armoured vehicle, we were still particularly vulnerable because we constituted such a significant threat.

As soon as the Daesh caught sight of our vehicle, we could well expect a large part of their weapons to direct fire at us.

After a 20-minute rest, and after reloading our weapons, the time had come to continue the battle.

On our way back into town we witnessed several more air raids. This time it was behind the town, in a south-westerly direction.

As the road from the south was close to where the Americans were bombing, I suspected they were attacking a convoy of vehicles on their way with reinforcements for the Daesh. This town was the last before the Iraqi border, where the Daesh had their stronghold. We knew the Daesh would defend the town fiercely – to the last man – as it was so strategically important to them.

We continued speeding along and we were now approaching the outskirts of the eastern part of the town.

I was sweating in the heavy gear. Lucky for me, it was getting cooler. The moon was still high, and the clear starry sky cast a wonderful glow over the landscape. Orion was in his usual position, and it looked as if Sagittarius was firing his arrow over us.

It was not hard to understand why religion plays such a big role down here. Anyone who gazed up at this amazing sky each night had to wonder about its meaning. With these spectacular stars as witnesses, the notion of a higher power did not seem so strange.

The red tracer shells were still being fired rapidly from our batteries from around the town. I was curling my toes, fearing that they might not see us in the dark and hit us.

We veered off in a westerly direction along the northern part of the town. We headed directly towards the shots coming from our own heavy machine guns, Dushka, which were still firing at the Daesh inside the town. If we continued along this path any longer, we would almost certainly be hit. The large 23mm shells would pierce us exactly where our armor was weakest – at the back.

"Fuck!" I shouted at Soran: "Stop the vehicle!" He immediately gave the order to the driver. The armoured vehicle jerked to a halt. Soran looked at me, puzzled. I made hand signals that imitated flying projectiles, and said: "Dushka." He instantly understood my point, took the radio, and gave the order for them to cease fire until further notice.

We changed direction and continued along the trenches that the Daesh had dug around the town to prevent any incursion of their positions.

As I had the most commanding view from the tower of the armoured vehicle, I made sure I constantly scanned the area for any hazards.

We approached a small bridge on the western side of the town. The bridge was the only route into the village.

Earlier, we had received reports that three of our own had been killed when they stepped on and detonated a mine. This was the huge explosion that I had heard previously. An alarming thought suddenly popped into my head: Why had the Daesh not mined or blown up the bridge? After all, it was the only crossing over their protective moat – from the east, north and west?

The vehicle was now only a few meters from the bridge. One thing seemed almost certain to me: They had mined the bridge that we were crossing. *It had to be mined.* Anything else made no sense. We were already on the first section of the bridge. We had to cross it if we were to attack the Daesh effectively inside the town. But if we were blown up now, we didn't stand a chance of continuing the battle.

I yelled to Soran: "Stop!"

The vehicle drew to a sudden halt. The fronts of the armoured vehicle's wheel-belts were already on the bridge. Soran gave me another quizzical look.

"The bridge is mined!" I shouted, above the clatter of the engine.

"Mine! Mine!" Soran looked startled. I made a hand gesture, signaling that we needed to reverse. The vehicle started moving again, backing up slightly.

We were still being shot at from different positions inside the town. I had to keep ducking my head as the bullets hit in and around the tower like hail on a car roof. I felt confident that they didn't have any weapons heavier than 12.7 mm, which the armoured vehicle could withstand. But I also knew that they still had RPG rockets. If they also had armor-piercing RPGs we stood little chance of survival – if they hit us.

It was dangerous to remain stationary for any length of time. Very dangerous. Our best defense against RPG rockets was to keep moving. But we had little room to maneuver. On one side was the trench; on the other was a steep incline that our vehicle could not climb.

On our starboard side was a large electricity pylon. We reversed toward the pylon to turn back in a north-easterly direction. As we came closer, I noticed several large thick cables hanging down from its mast. Before I could shout to stop, we drove into the cables, which became entangled in our wheel-belts. FUCK AGAIN! If we got stuck now, we would be easy prey for the RPGs, especially as we had our side turned towards the enemy. The front of an armoured vehicle is made of the thickest steel. The sides are less well protected and, on top of that, the sides provide a bigger and broader target for an RPG gunner.

"Drive the other way!" I shouted to Soran, who passed on my order to the driver.

While I looked uneasily at the thick steel cables that ran under the belts, we started moving forward. If we got stuck, our nearest cover would be the trench near the bridge. If the steel cables became tangled in our belt-wheels, under no circumstances could we remain in the vehicle.

We would be 10 combatants grouped on a few square meters: the worst case scenario when faced with enemy fire. If this happened, we would have to evacuate the armoured vehicle as quickly as possible and take cover in the trench. It was hardly an ideal situation to remain in the trench. The Daesh could bombard us from several directions. Nor could we retreat, because the area behind us did not offer any cover.

As the armoured vehicle moved cautiously forward, the cables remained flat on the ground behind us. I breathed a sigh of utter relief. We proceeded about a hundred meters in a northerly direction. I could see where muzzle flash was coming from a building. I returned fire.

Heval Shingal changed from the RPG to a PKC machine gun (nicknamed *PIXIE*), of which we had several in our vehicle. Each time he fired it behind me, it gave me a shock. The PKC makes a terrible racket, especially if – like me – you are sitting only two meters in front of it. Shingal was shooting on the starboard side close to the tower where I was sitting, which threw the din of his firing directly at my neck.

I had started using earplugs to filter out the worse noise, to protect my hearing. I had had ringing in my left ear for days. It was shots blasted from a Dushka that had caused my tinnitus. I wanted to prevent any further damage to my hearing by using these earplugs. If I did not press them in to the bottom of my ear, they let in most sounds, but removed the loudest noises.

I had discovered an additional benefit of ear plugs: using them made me calmer and let me fight with greater focus. Hearing is a sense that can affect the psyche enormously. By removing the worst noise made by the weapons, everything seems less violent, so it's possible to act with greater calm and with a cool head.

Suddenly the whistle of rockets started again. But it was different to the sound of RPGs. Brilliant white sparks that looked like fireworks came from the town centre, during which several smaller explosions could be heard.

This was something new! What was it?

At first I thought it was planes that had launched some advanced form of ammunition. It continued for some time, followed by a pause. Then came the sound of rockets ... *SSSHHHsss*... and again. Each detonation was followed by white sparks that shot up like fireworks from the ground and from the houses in the town. They hit exactly the spot where a large portion of the Daesh's forces were fighting. We were happy to see any attacks that supported us.

Soran stuck his head up through the hatch and told me, "YPG rockets." I now knew from which vehicle the rockets came. I had noticed this vehicle carrying a battery of rockets on several occasions. The rockets were mounted on the back of a pickup truck and had four pipes in three rows. They were fired by connecting the wires of a car battery to the rockets. We had built rockets like these ourselves. But I had never seen their impact from such close quarters. What an impressive spectacle it was.

The Daesh were scattered throughout the town and fought fiercely. The air attacks had far from annihilated them. Nothing in this battle had yet been decided. It could take weeks to defeat the Daesh, especially if they got supplies into Shingal from the south.

I had previously suggested to Soran that we should send a patrol south of the town along the mountain ridge. They should move forward unseen from RV point to RV point (rendezvous) and finally establish an OP (observation post) with a good view from the mountain ridge down to the supply road. They should then observe enemy movements over a period of time, jot down everything they saw, and report back. At the same time they should make a *range card*, which is a detailed outline of the terrain, documenting all the important details about the landscape. Distances were important. This range card could later be used to launch an attack against supply vehicles.

We had exactly the right people to perform this task. My old team, with which I first arrived in Iraq, were still at the western front. We had already carried out similar missions. I knew they would be only too happy to help us with this patrolling task. There were several SF (Special Forces) on my old team. Their talent was wasted on the western front because it involved immobile trench warfare without many attacks.

When I realized that the war out there would remain static, and that we would not see much action, I asked for a transfer from the western front.

However, it was too late for that solution now. Before we had time to get a patrol on the move, American aircrafts had attacked and we had already entered the city.

We headed towards the northern part of the town, and again I heard the frightening sound of a rocket ... *SSSHHHsss.* The rocket flew directly toward us. I ducked, held fast, and prepared myself for the descent and detonation. It was a close shave and the rocket landed right next to us with a huge explosion. Soil and stones were thrown into the air and landed on the vehicle. It was pouring soil and sand down my head, and I could feel the stones hit my helmet.

The driver had also seen the rocket through his hatch. Now he sped up and started to zigzag, as if he expected another rocket. He seemed to be panic-stricken. I think he was more concerned about looking out for another rocket than keeping an eye on where he was going. In the darkness he did not notice that he was about to drive directly into a small outbuilding. He only discovered it at the last minute. As he turned sharply to the right, he went directly into a small ditch. The vehicle hit the ground at the bottom of the trench, and we flew forward. Several hevals rolled around on top of each other as the armoured vehicle came to an abrupt halt.

I was still standing on the tower and was thrown around. I screamed in pain as my back knocked into an iron bar in the tower. Soran had heard my screams and now looked uneasily at me. I was writhing on the ground and grasped my back in pain. But there was neither time nor space for worrying about pain. All that counted now was survival. The driver tried to reverse out of the trench. The diesel engine next to me revved up, sending noise and smoke into the armoured vehicle. The clutch smelt burnt. But the belt-wheels of the vehicle just spun round and round in the sandy ditch. The driver looked frantic. If he had appeared to be panicking earlier, he was now about to explode in desperation.

The RPG-shooter who had nearly hit us earlier was almost certainly reloading and ready to fire another rocket at us at anytime.

There was nothing we could do. The armoured vehicle was stuck and unable to free itself.

"Dismount! Evacuate!" I yelled, and crawled behind the vehicle, past the crates of ammunition. Sometimes I would get stuck in the narrow passage that runs from the cab to the back of the vehicle because, as part of my rig, I had Kalash-magazines, grenades and knives mounted on my upper body.

You never knew if you would suddenly need to vacate the vehicle. It was therefore necessary to always wear full battle gear – even inside the vehicle.

Soran was on the radio and had already started requesting the other armoured vehicle, which normally moved with us, to come and pull us out.

From time to time we heard the sound of bullets hitting the vehicle. We now had to risk going out in the open and away from the protection of the armoured vehicle. Deep anxiety was seen and felt amongst all aboard. We opened the hatches on the back, and all jumped out at the same time.

We ran behind the vehicle, away from the Daesh's positions, and used it as cover. We divided ourselves into two fire teams, with five in each, to defend ourselves more effectively. It was dangerous remaining behind the vehicle, as it attracted far too much enemy fire.

There was a house just meters away from us, which seemed to offer the most obvious protection. As the first team ran towards the building, the second team fired at the enemy. I rested the PKC light machine gun on the vehicle, which had now slid further down the ditch. I fired while the first team was running.

    I could still feel the pain in my back, but tried to ignore it. Every now and then a spasm shot through my back. I found it hard to remain upright. I was swearing and firing at the same time. I could not see exactly where the Daesh were. But I had a good idea of their position, so I kept firing at the building, which was only about 75 meters away. And, sure enough: suddenly I saw muzzle flash coming from the house. They fired at us. The bullets whistled above our heads, hit the ground, and kicked up dust. Some hit the vehicle.

    It is dangerous to use a hard surface for cover because the projectiles can skim cross it or shatter and turn into shrapnel. This has given rise to the expression: "Aim small and miss small." If one shoots too high, one will certainly hit nothing but fresh air. But by shooting low, the bullet can still hit the enemy by ricocheting off a hard surface. If one is firing using an automatic weapon, it gradually drifts up and hits the enemy.

    I wanted to get away from the vehicle as soon as possible, before the next RPG was fired. I was just about to shout for the first team to cover us while we ran for shelter. But this was unnecessary, as they were already firing with all their weapons.

We raced as fast as we could towards the house, with bullets flying around our ears. A heval screamed as he was hit in the arm by a bullet, but he continued running and reached cover behind the building with the rest of us. Fortunately, it was only a graze. We were now on the northern side of the building.

I had earlier fired several hundred rounds with the PKC into this particular building, from which they had been shooting at us. There was not much chance of anyone inside the structure having survived. But, just to be certain, one heval threw a grenade into the house before we entered. The grenade made a massive blast when it detonated. I was pleased to have my ear protection.

We went in and found an enemy combatant lying on his back in the middle of the room. He was big and heavily built with a long black beard. He was the image of a typical terrorist. I knelt down beside him and shone my flashlight under him to look for any wires or booby-traps.

The Daesh sometimes put explosives on their corpses, which they know will be moved and buried. They sometimes even filled a corpse with explosives. **But** I could not see any mine. I touched his neck. He was still warm and was therefore hardly likely to have been booby-trapped.

The others took up positions at the window and the door. Heval Rosa sat down leaning against the wall, close to the body, and lit a cigarette. She pulled a couple of pillows towards her and patted them. It was a sign to me that I should sit down next to her. She knew that I had hurt my back and tried to be helpful.

I sat down, and she offered me a cigarette, which I took and managed to light. There was something special about a uniformed woman with a machine gun. By now I had been in the same *tabur* (platoon/unit) as Rosa for a long time, and even though she was rarely in the armoured vehicle, I saw her almost daily. She always smiled and laughed a lot, which I encouraged by making all sorts of funny faces.

I also tried to make the other young hevals laugh, not only Rosa. And it was not difficult, since they all had a good sense of humor. I had inherited a special pair of thumbs that I could bend backwards more than 90 degrees. If I did this at the same time as I moved my eyebrows up and down quickly, the young hevals would break out in giggles and sometimes could not stop laughing. The shortest distance between two people is a smile. It was fun to play the clown sometimes, and it took our minds off the war.

But now the situation was anything but comical. We were caught close to a strong Daesh position with limited supplies of ammunition and water. If we could not get the vehicle pulled free, we were in serious trouble. I tried to cheer everyone up by pointing to the dead Daesh's feet and holding my nose, as if his feet smelt. The others laughed, and it helped a little to lighten our mood.

Soran came into the room, looked around in the darkness, and saw the shadowy figure lying on the floor. He walked over and shouted at the dead Daesh – which he apparently thought was a heval sleeping or resting – and ordered him to stand up and fight. He gave him a gentle kick. We all broke out laughing.

"He is dead," I said.

"Dead?" Asked Soran.

"Yes, it's a dead Daesh."

"Good!" said Soran, and went to the window to get a good view to assess the situation.

While I was sitting next to Rosa near the dead Daesh, a thought suddenly entered my head: You are dreaming! This is too unreal to be happening. A few months ago I had been at home, where all was peace and harmony, and now here was a dead terrorist lying on the floor in front of me? We actually laughed about his smelly feet while we smoked a cigarette? Was there really a beautiful young girl of only 18 years in camouflage uniform with pink sneakers and a machine gun sitting beside me, while there were shots flying in and out the window?

I wanted to pinch myself to see if it was all really real.

It was real. These things were happening around me, right now. I began to think back to the day, last year, when Yana Fayed had called me at home. It was the day that started everything which changed my life forever.

2. Yana and Anas

8 Months Earlier

It was a summer afternoon. I had just come home from work when the phone rang. I was surprised to hear Yana Fayed's voice. She was obviously distressed and spoke in broken English. I had to ask her to speak more slowly and clearly. It had been several months since I was last in touch with Yana's husband, Anas.

I had met Anas Fayed for the first time thirteen years earlier. He was a principal at a train station just outside Aleppo in Syria, where I had been based as a service technician.

Every morning Anas would invite me for tea at the station. He was an exceptionally hospitable and friendly man. He was also intelligent and very outgoing. Anas also had a great sense of humor, and we laughed together a lot. After a few months we had become close friends, and Anas invited me home to meet his family: his wife Yana, and their four children aged two to thirteen years.

Like Anas, Yana was friendly and welcoming. I had expected people in Syria to be conservative Muslims who wore *hijab* or *burqa*, and who did not tolerate other religions. But, to my surprise, there was a large Christian population and many churches in Aleppo. Women were often fashionably dressed, with Gucci bags and sunglasses. They listened to American rock music and drank wine. I was surprised, all in all, at how progressive Aleppo was. Yana, being Muslim, made me ashamed of my prejudices. I was delighted that I had been proven wrong.

Whenever I had needed a bit of help with something, Anas was always there for me. I remember one time when I had lifted some heavy spare parts and hurt my back. Anas drove me to the hospital and made sure that I received proper care. Nearly every day during the week that I was hospitalized, Anas would come and visit me, bringing newspapers and magazines, and homemade food from Yana.

It was sometimes hard working all over the world, as I often did for long periods. At times I would feel isolated and lonely, far away from friends and family. If Anas noticed that I'd had a bad day, he would lift my mood with his colorful personality and cheerfulness. Even after I had completed my assignment in Syria, I travelled back to Aleppo to visit Anas and Yana.

Anas was the best friend that one could wish for; and I loved him like a brother.

I was wondering about Yana's call.

Her voice sounded frantic when she told me that some men had come and taken Anas away. At first I couldn't understand what she meant?

"Taken him? Where? "I asked.

She told me that they had decided to move with the children to her sister's home, in a part of Aleppo that was safer, once Assad's forces started dropping barrel bombs. They had been sitting and eating dinner when three men with weapons suddenly stormed into the apartment and had forced Anas to go with them at gunpoint.

Yana's desperation started rubbing off on me, and I also began to get anxious.

"When did you last hear from Anas?" I asked.

"It was nine days ago," said Yana.

I felt shocked, and didn't know how to comfort Yana, or how I could help.

In the following days I called Yana regularly to find out if there were any new developments about Anas and his whereabouts. After several weeks without news of Anas, I could barely bear calling Yana. It was agonizing to hear her cry without being able to do anything to help. I promised Yana that I'd keep in touch. But I didn't call as often anymore. I felt cowardly and ashamed of not being able to do anything.

I had never been in such a situation before. Nor had I ever felt so helpless and inept.

It was several months before I heard from Syria again. This time it was not Yana, but her sister who rang. She told me that Yana had travelled to Iraq with the children, and that they were now staying in a refugee camp near Erbil. I asked her to ask Yana to contact me when she heard from her, so that I could send them some money.

The weeks went by and I heard nothing from Syria.

I had followed the war in Syria from the start. The war had taken an unexpected turn. IS had suddenly appeared on the scene out of the ashes of the Iraq war. Every day I followed the accounts of their attacks against the civilian population, and my indignation grew. For me, it was personal. Often I could recognize places in Aleppo from the pictures.

For me, it was not a distant war in a distant land. It was about my friends. They had treated me like family, and it was therefore also about them being *my* family. And it was not just Yana and Anas that I cared about. It was the Syrian people.

Once, I had walked into a hairdresser in Aleppo for a haircut.

It was a time when I still got value for money when having a haircut (before my hair had done me the favor of falling out so that I no longer needed to shampoo and comb it – or have it cut!) The hairdresser was very friendly, and he spent almost 45 minutes cutting my hair while his son trimmed my nails. When I wanted to pay and leave, he refused to accept my money. I was taken aback. He had spent almost an hour cutting a stranger's hair, and did not want to be paid for his work?

"You are a guest in my country," said the hairdresser. "It is free for you."

Exceptionally hospitable and friendly: that is what the Syrians are. It was impossible to just look on passively while the Daesh or Assad killed these innocent people.

In the weeks that followed, I started to investigate how I could support Yana and her children, and how I could support the fight against the Daesh.

I quickly found out that those who were most worth fighting for – and with – were the Kurds. Shortly afterwards, I bought a ticket and flew via Istanbul to Erbil. I had already checked around and, through Facebook, I had made a few contacts in Erbil who were willing to help me with my chores. I booked a room at *Hotel Istanbul*, feeling sure that the Daesh would never bomb a hotel with a name like that. Turkey was, after all, known for its support for the Daesh.

It was from Yana's sister that I had learned that Yana and the children were staying in a camp, an hour's drive east of Erbil. A few days after I had arrived in Erbil, I met my Kurdish contact, Hemn, and we had dinner together. Hemn said that he would be happy to drive me up to the refugee camp. He was a young man in his late twenties. He had recently lost his job and therefore had plenty of time on his hands. I didn't get the impression that he lacked for money. He drove in a big, expensive car, wore modern clothes, and from what I could see from his Facebook page, he also travelled a lot. South Kurdistan was a wealthy area with a population that had gradually grown into a large affluent middle class.

The next morning we set off to the UNICEF camp, which was located just inland, in the mountains east of Erbil. After a good hour's drive, we arrived at the camp. Hemn parked the car outside, and we asked the guard for Yana Fayed. The guard checked our IDs, and we were told that she lived in a tent a few minutes' walk from the guard's post. I had brought a thousand US dollars with me and an extra suitcase filled with warm clothes for the children. Fortunately, I had kept the winter clothes that my daughter had grown out of. I had also visited a second hand clothes shop and bought three more warm jackets.

I had not seen Yana and Anas for four years, but I had kept in touch with them via Facebook and Skype. I wondered how she would react when she saw me, and what shape she and the children would be in.

The camp was well organized, and although the circumstances were extreme, they at least had food, water and electricity. There were about 500 large blue tents in the camp. Dirt roads and muddy tracks ran between the tents. You mostly saw women and children. If you happened to see an occasional single man, they were usually old. I assumed that the men were either dead or fighting in the war. A whole generation was growing up without fathers, grandfathers, uncles or brothers. It was a depressing thought.

I saw a sad looking little girl outside the tent. She seemed to resemble Anas' second youngest daughter, but I wasn't sure.

"Yana?" I said to the girl, and she pointed into the tent.

I stuck my head inside and said, "Hello."

A woman who was busy cleaning up turned towards me. It was Yana.

"Jørgen?" Said Yana, surprised.

We embraced each other. Yana started crying, but quickly dried her tears and invited us inside.

She looked old and tired. She had deep, dark rings under her eyes, as if she had been crying for a long time. Which she had.

I introduced Hemn, and we sat down at a small table. Yana made us tea. There was silence for a while. Then Yana began to tell us what had happened in Erbil. She explained how they had abducted Anas.

"He is dead," she said. "I know he's dead."

She was probably right. There was not much hope that Anas was alive. If he was, Anas would have contacted his family long ago. The Daesh took no prisoners unless they had "value", political or financial. The mood inside the tent was gloomy.

I gave Yana the money and clothes. I promised that I would keep in touch.

We went for a walk around the camp with Yana and saw many tragedies. Orphaned children with clothes in tatters were rummaging through a pile of garbage. Others came to beg for money. I gave a couple of kids five-dollar notes. One little boy was so pleased to get the $5 that he ran away happily, flapping his little arms like a bird.

I thought of my own daughter. I wanted her to witness this misery so that she would never forget just how privileged she was. I wanted her to remain humble so that she would never take her own good fortune for granted.

We continued our walk around the camp. As we made our way back to Yanas' tent, I kept wondering about these people's fate. We had more tea and talked for a few hours. I tried my best to instill Yana with courage and hope. As it began to get dark, we said farewell to Yana and drove back towards Erbil. I was relieved to get out from the camp. It was hard to be there. It was easier to breathe outside the camp. Still, I decided to stay on in Erbil for a couple more weeks and regularly visit Yana and the children. In the meantime, I decided to seek admission into the Peshmerga – a Kurdish military unit.

3. Asayish: The Secret Police

Having seen the victims of war with my own eyes in the refugee camp, I was even more determined to support the fight against the Daesh. Not least because of my family, I didn't want to fight on the front line as a soldier. It was too dangerous. I was hoping that the Kurdish Peshmerga army could use my technical skills, and that I could support their fight in that way.

By now I had been in Erbil for two weeks, trying in vain to get in touch with Peshmerga. According to the Kurdish web page on the Internet, volunteers had to contact the police in Erbil. They would assist by referring volunteers to the Peshmerga. I left the hotel to find a taxi. The police station was about ten minutes drive away. I asked the taxi driver to stop at the shopping centre Mega Mall. I had seen on the map that there was a large police station behind the mall. I went to a petrol station, which was between the mall and the police, and continued toward the entrance of the police station.

It was autumn. But for me, who was used to the cold North, it was still warm. While the locals were wearing thick jackets, I wore only a thin sweater. Three armed guards stood outside the police station. When they saw me walk straight towards them, they gripped their Kalashnikov rifles – preparing themselves for action. There had been regular terrorist attacks in the Kurdish part of Iraq, including here in Erbil.

They looked tense as they followed me with their eyes. They were not used to seeing foreigners. Western tourists were more or less non-existent in Erbil, the city called Hewlêr in the local dialect. The few foreigners who stayed here were working mainly in the oil business, and they never walked around alone on foot.

I tried to talk to the guards in English, but they did not understand me; something I was used to.

I continued with my sign language: "I join Peshmerga."

To help explain myself better, I always carried pictures on my phone. So I showed them one of me in uniform. After they had finished searching my small backpack, they seemed more relaxed. Realizing that I had come to offer my help, they greeted me politely.

By making a phone sign, I tried to ask them to call someone who understood and spoke English. They called someone and I explained: "I am here to join the Peshmerga. Can I speak to the captain, please?"

They were just about to lead me into the police station, but they wanted me to leave my rucksack outside at the entrance. When I insisted on taking it in with me, they allowed me to do so.

We went inside and into an office. They offered me a seat on a large leather sofa. The room was tiled, and a long fluorescent light threw off a bright clinical light. They brought me some tea; a common courtesy in this very hospitable part of the world. Minutes later, an officer in a blue uniform with silver stripes on his epaulets came in. He gave me a questioning look.

I began using sign language again, trying to explain that I was keen to join Peshmerga as a volunteer soldier. Along with my educational certificates, I showed him photos to indicate that I was an engineer and had been a soldier.

After some time, another officer – with even more silver stripes on his shoulders – came in and showed me into another room. As he sat himself down behind a large dark desk, he asked me to take a seat. He was the station's captain and Chief of Police.

I was served some more tea.

After some time, a plain-clothes criminal detective joined us. He spoke good English, as well as German. As I have lived in both Germany and Switzerland, and was fluent in German, we continued our conservation in this language. He, like many other Kurds, had lived in Germany, but had returned to Iraq when the Kurdish region gained its autonomy and economic conditions had improved.

The plain-clothes officer asked me why I had visited the police station. While I explained, he translated to the captain. When it dawned on the captain that I had come to help them in the war against IS, he got up, walked around the desk, grabbed me by the shoulders and kissed me on both cheeks.

The captain then spoke and the officer translated. He said, "You are our brother, and we thank you for coming all this way to help us. We are very grateful." He went back behind the desk, took out his cell phone, and started calling around.

In the meantime, I was served with more tea.

Apart from the glaring white light shining from the fluorescent tubes, it was all very nice and pleasant. On the wall hung a landscape painting of the mountains that border Turkey, Iran and Iraq, which have – through the ages – offered the Kurds the possibilities of escape. It was a saying that "the mountains are the Kurds' only friend." I pondered the many decades during which the Kurds had been persecuted by various governments in the Middle East. I was happy that it was specifically the Kurds that I could fight with. They were not only tolerant towards other religions, but were not as fanatical about many other things as other countries in the region.

The police chief saw me admiring the beautiful painting and, through the interpreter, said: "I paint, it calms me down. I want you to have this painting as a 'thank you' because you have travelled so far to help us." But I haven't helped anybody yet, I thought. Not wanting to appear discourteous by rejecting his gracious offer, I politely accepted his gift. "When the war is over, you can come and get it," he continued. "OK, that's a deal," I replied.

We waited a little longer, and the phone rang.

The Chief answered and said: "Ok. Aha, hm,", and hung up.

Through the interpreter, he addressed me again: "I'm sorry, my friend, but I cannot help you. You have to go to the Peshmerga Ministry." But I was not going to let myself be dismissed so easily. "Is there absolutely nothing you can do?" I asked. I knew that personal references meant everything in the Middle East, and that if I was sent off with the blessing of the head of police, it would certainly be easier to open doors.

"I'm sorry," he said.

We drank our tea, and I talked a little with the plain-clothes officer about his time in Germany.

Suddenly it seemed as if the Chief had changed his mind, or remembered something. He pulled out his phone, made a short call, and spoke to me again.

"My friend will come and collect you shortly," said the police chief. This was good news, and I thanked him.

More tea was served while we waited.

After approximately half an hour, two men in long black leather jackets arrived. In a way, they were reminiscent of the Gestapo. They spoke briefly with the Chief and asked me to come with them. We left the police station and got into a Toyota pickup.

It was now dark and cold outside. It was November, and winter was slowly approaching. We drove off through the lit streets of Erbil.

Both men had Kalashnikovs with them in the front of the car. One was tall with light skin; the other was short, stocky, and darker. Both men had moustaches, as men often do down here. It was rare to see Kurds with a beard – at least in these parts.

One of the men turned to me and said in broken English that I had to learn Kurdish if I was going to fight with them. I felt encouraged that he assumed that I was going to join them. I was looking forward to learning Kurdish, I replied. I had already learnt some of the very basics of the language, but hardly enough to hold a conversation in Kurdish.

We drove on for about 15 minutes in a westerly direction until we arrived at a large building complex.

We were checked at the entrance by sniffer dogs and men in Peshmerga uniforms. We continued past the entry guard and parked outside a large building. We got out, and the men motioned me to follow them. We entered a long corridor and made our way through the building for several minutes. It consisted mainly of offices. We eventually came out on the other side and went into a second, adjacent building, where a group of men were standing smoking cigarettes. There were both civilian and uniformed men.

A soldier came up to me and told me to raise my arms. He then body searched me and checked my bag. We left the tall and the short guy that had escorted me. I followed the soldier into a large meeting room, where about 20 men were seated in big comfy armchairs.

I knew, judging from the surroundings, that I had come into an area used by higher ranking officers. Maybe as high up as generals. There were also some men in suits. In the background was a modern flat screen showing news about the war. There were oriental carpets on the floors and plastic floral decorations on the walls. The room could just as well have been in a luxury hotel.

I felt humble amongst all these distinguished gentlemen; and slightly uncomfortable about disturbing them here in the middle of their war. They probably had more important things to do.

I took a seat near the entrance and was offered more tea. My bladder was about to burst.

After a few minutes, a gentleman asked me in fluent English what I had to offer Peshmerga. He had apparently already heard that I had come as a volunteer soldier and a technical specialist. I explained that I had had military training, and that I also had many years of experience as a technician. The man then turned to two plain-clothes men who sat a bit further away in the room. They got up, came towards me, and asked me to follow them into another room.

When we reached the office, they asked me to take a seat. One of the two, who I would later get to know as Colonel Mahir, sat down behind a large desk. He had a very calm and quiet demeanor, and seemed nice and approachable. He was handsome, neatly dressed in a suit and tie, and probably in his mid-forties. The other man seemed less friendly. He was also dressed in a suit, but less stylish than Mahir. He appeared altogether rougher, like a tough criminal detective.

He began asking me a lot of questions. Friendly, but very direct. They both spoke fluent English and had obviously lived abroad. It is common that intelligence officers have higher education, and these two gentlemen were no exception.

I christened the rough hewn man Ivan, as I didn't remember his name. It was obvious that Ivan had been used to interrogate al Qaeda terrorists – the hard way. Torture is not uncommon in Iraq. I certainly had no intention of becoming enemies with this man. And there was no reason to. I had come to help, and they treated me with respect.

Ivan asked about my background: both military and civilian. I willingly gave him an account about my past, and made sure that I showed them all my documents. Mahir nodded occasionally with a friendly smile. Ivan asked me why I thought that I, being a foreigner, could just come and expect to be accepted into their army. Would it have been possible, he asked, for him to travel to Europe, show up in the barracks, and expect to become a soldier? "My country is not at war", I replied, "and does not have the same need for well-trained soldiers."

"Hmm ...," growled Ivan.

More tea was served.

I had already drunk several liters that day, but I drank on politely. Several decades of travelling around the world had taught me never to dismiss a country's customs, but to follow them. I always accept food and drink, even if sometimes it was not to my taste. Generally, however, I relish eating all kinds of food.

After World War II, my parents had grown up with very meager resources. By today's standard, they would have both been considered poor when they were children. They had taught us not to be picky and to eat everything, from livers and hearts and pig's tails to goats and yellow peas. Once, I copied my father's example and sucked out the head of a boiled cod, including its eyes. I never repeated this. It was better to just accept everything that was served, and just nibble at what one didn't like. Even if you don't particularly like something, it is good manners to accept it.

There is an ocean of unwritten rules around the world that are important to follow. Amongst the Kurds, I would later learn – amongst others rules – not to cross my legs, not to swear, and not to show too much skin when ladies are present. Good manners and common sense are universal.

My father had been an officer in the navy and an instructor at the diving school in the old days.

Discipline was strict, and he had taught us to always be polite and well mannered.

The interrogation continued. They asked me how I thought I could be useful in both a civilian and military way.

I had spent several years in military training and had done quite well in the army. I had used weapons since my childhood. I did well in shooting competitions and I had later competed with rifles.

I had grown up in the countryside on an island in southern Scandinavia. My family had a horse stud farm, and 17 acres of apple trees. Since the age of six, my elder brother and I had tended the orchard. It was not fun having to work every day after school. But now, in hindsight, I can see the benefits. We also had lots of fun with various agricultural machines, such as tractors and small trucks, which I learned to operate before I could reach the pedals. I had to stand up to drive the tractor.

My childhood home was right next to water and forests. I especially loved the forest, its smells and sounds. I went into the forest nearly every day; at least in the summer. We rode our horses into the water and we had built a sling so that we could swing out into the water from the escarpment. I soon developed a natural sense of being and moving in nature, which often benefitted me in the military.

I knew that it was not this part of my past that would arouse my interrogators' interest. But I had a small ace up my sleeve, which I believed would make them listen more carefully. It was that my real interest was not shooting weapons. As a technician, it was the physics behind the weapons that interested me most. For me, a weapon was an excellent way to demonstrate the laws of physics and chemistry.

The way weapons work not only contains Einstein's and Newton's theories in practice, but also a wealth of physics, chemistry, and other laws. In particular, there are aspects of thermodynamics that weapons and combustion engines have in common. My professional field of specialty is combustion engines. I had noticed that the silencing and cooling of hot gases had a common denominator. In the same way, one could cool the gases that are released by a weapon when a projectile is fired.

A few years earlier I had used this knowledge to build and patent a new type of suppressor valve at the "Institutes Für Geistiges Eigentum".

If there was anything that can arouse the interest of governments at war, it is weapons technology. Even a small and simple design like a suppressor was of interest to the intelligence services in the war against Al Qaeda and IS.

I took out a machine drawing that I had used to build a prototype, and showed it to the two agents. Colonel Mahir listened attentively. Ivan was less impressed.

He continued: "It's illegal to make such a device."

"No, it isn't," I said.

"It's illegal to make a weapon silencer," repeated Ivan.

"There is no such thing as a weapon silencer," I replied. "It's called a suppressor because it only suppresses the sound. It doesn't silence it."

"It's illegal either way you put it," said Ivan.

"Well, I have a manufacturer's license from the local authorities in my country of residence allowing me to build a prototype."

Mahir interjected: "Can you build one for us?"

"Yes, I can. That's easy," I replied.

We continued talking for a while. When we finished, Mahir said: "I will get my driver to take you to the hotel, and we can talk later."

The driver was summoned, we shook hands, and I followed the army driver out to the colonel's big Jeep Cherokee.

When I arrived at the hotel, I walked through the reception and up to my room. I felt that the staff looked at me differently compared to when I first arrived. The staff had no doubt noticed all the military equipment in my room.

I had been out to eat *shawarma* with a Canadian-Kurdish contact a few days earlier. He also worked in the security services. He told me that one day he had seen a soldier in an altercation with another man. The soldier pulled the man to the ground and shot him three times in the chest with his Kalash. People, he said, walked past as if nothing had happened.

I understood perfectly that soldiers in these parts of the world are respected and feared. On the whole, a heavy atmosphere pervaded Kurdistan; which was not surprising considering that the country was at war. You did not notice it at first. But everybody was personally involved in the war or had family that was. The Kurds shouldered it bravely, even with a smile, as if it was normal – which it was for them. But if you sat in a café and smoked a hookah, and looked more closely, you could sense the tension beneath the surface.

I lay on my bed in the hotel room and wrote in my diary. I had to go to the toilet several times because of the amount of tea I had been drinking. I didn't want to wake up in the middle of the night and disturb my sleep by having to go to the toilet. While the local imam sang his prayers from the mosque around the corner, I tucked into some nuts from the mini-bar.

I had studied Muhammad and his life. He seemed alright; though religion was not my cup of tea. I couldn't grasp why people got themselves so worked up over that kind of stuff. When one has lived abroad for a long time, one knows that people are the same everywhere on earth. I felt ashamed about the West's ignorance and fear of Muslims. It was not Muslims one should fear; in the same way that one should not fear Christians. But both Muslims and Christians could be fascists, fanatics, extremists and many other things. Was this so hard to understand?

We northerners had once suffered the same fate. Hundreds of different Germanic peoples had once been labeled 'barbarians' – as one and the same. Back then it was the Romans who were prejudiced and ignorant. Maybe we were all the same? Yes, to some extent, but as individuals, *very* different.

More than anything else, the Daesh is basically fascist. That they happen to live in a Muslim country and used Islam as a rallying point, is secondary. You had to look into the human mind if you wanted to see behind the veils of the conflicts. It is only when one knows what a man wants, that one knows the man.

Baghdadi and Saddam's generals primarily wanted revenge against the Americans, as well as power, recognition, and status. Ideas like religion are abstract, and the human brain may have difficulty relating to ideology. Baghdadi had studied theology in Baghdad after he had been rejected by the law school because of poor grades. Later, he was arrested by the Americans during the Iraq war in the 2000s. In prison at Camp Bucca he met Saddam's generals and the Islamists, who would later form the rest of the IS leadership.

When one begins to notice how history repeats itself again and again, like the earth turning 'round and 'round the sun, one cannot help but become aware of the similarities. It was in many ways similar to Germany during the Weimar Republic. If society is not sufficiently developed to counter it, people will be people, and sooner or later a new Idi Amin, Hitler or Pol Pot will appear.

The next morning I got up, did some exercises, and washed myself to the sound of prayers coming from the mosque. I dressed in a polo shirt and khaki trousers, which is a universal way of dressing anywhere in the Middle East and for all occasions. I took the stairway to the seventh floor and walked into the restaurant. As I always left a small tip, I was given first class service. This day was no exception. The waiter, a young man, stood poised to make sure that I was quickly served with all the necessities.

I have lived much of my life abroad and see a tip as a mixture of a sign of respect and charity – as wages are often miserable. The good service is just an extra bonus. Having lived in hotels so much, I've had to learn how to feel at home in them. This included some routines, such as asking waiters to reserve the same table for me. In this way, I needn't look for a new place every day, and could at least sit in familiar surroundings – of a sort.

I made sure that I got some milk and yogurt in my stomach before I drank the acidy coffee.

After breakfast I went back to my room and brushed my teeth. I left the room and walked through the lobby out to the front of the hotel and waved for a taxi. I was accustomed to taxi drivers not understanding what I said, so I always had at least a word or phrase ready to describe my destination.

Once, when I worked for the American Defense Forces in Bahrain, a taxi driver dropped me off at the wrong naval base – where I was almost shot! I had approached the reception at the base, but was told that the ship I was looking for was not there. I had then gone outside and tried to call my agent, who had forgotten to pick me up at the airport. A US marine had seen me talking on the phone and had suspected that I could be coordinating an attack. He had swung his heavy machine gun around so that it aimed straight at me. He had armed the gun and shouted that I should drop the phone. Which I did immediately. A 0.5" heavy machine gun can make some nasty holes in people, or rather, rip them to pieces.

A taxi stopped, and I got in. I simply said: "Asayish Headquarters," to the driver. Everyone in Erbil knew what Asayish was.

I was dropped off at the main entrance and immediately I was monitored carefully by the guards. There had been numerous bomb attacks on Asayish over the years. I went into a waiting room and explained that I had come to see Captain Kameran. I was not the only one apparently. I was required to first see Colonel Mahir. I was shown into the colonel's office and offered coffee and water.

Mahir was a busy man. The regular police in Erbil were not the most trusted, and many important issues were sorted out here at Asayish. A stream of different kinds of people went in and out of Mahirs office: from peasants in sandals with scarf on their head (that looked as if they had just parked their sheep at the entrance), to distinguished gentlemen in suits. Although I did not understand much of what was said, the meaning was clear: Mahir got things sorted out, and also served as a kind of judge.

Here in Erbil there was a relaxed attitude to the separation of executive and judicial powers, at least for minor cases. I was in no hurry, and it was interesting to follow the daily business inside Colonel Mahirs office. I knew that patience was respected as a virtue. Occasionally, Mahir offered me a cigarette with a friendly smile. I was brought tea at regular intervals as a couple of hours passed away.

A large flat screen hung on the wall. Several of the guests in Mahirs office were watching it, following the fighting on the front only a few kilometers from Erbil. I was not quite sure why I had to be present at the many meetings in Mahirs posh office. I felt that it was probably a sign of respect and trust that I was privy to his meetings, so I said nothing.

After some time Mahir addressed me. "Captain Kameran is coming to collect you soon." Shortly afterwards, a young gentleman in his late twenties came in and asked me to follow him to his office. His office was just a few meters down the hall on the opposite side. Kameran's office was less stylish than Mahirs.

Two other men in suits, who were sitting there, stood up and gave me a friendly greeting.

Kameran asked me to take a seat on the chair opposite his desk.

He took out a piece of paper and began to ask in fluent English about my background and training. Later I found out that Kameran had a university degree from Salahaddin University in Erbil. The university had been named after the famous Salahaddin, who fought against the Crusaders and was respected by allies and enemies alike. Alongside Apo, Salahaddin was probably the most famous Kurd who ever lived.

They didn't have any computers in the office, only smartphones, which were eagerly used to access the Internet. With Captain Kameran having to write everything down by hand and translating my background from English into Kurdish, I foresaw a long day ahead. With my many years of working experience, Kameran would not be writing down a short CV.

Kameran was like Mahir; a calm type, who seemed mature despite his relatively young age. I soon took a liking to Kameran. After a few hours of being interviewed, and numerous cups of tea later, it finally seemed as though we had finished. To my great joy,

Kameran looked up and said: "Welcome to Peshmerga. You are the first foreigner to join the Peshmerga."

This sounded good. Really good. After I had witnessed the misery in the refugee camps in Iraq, this is what I had been striving towards. Kameran called the driver. We agreed to meet the next day, and I was once again on my way back to the hotel.

The next day, Kameran phoned to say that my admission was still not guaranteed. First we had to talk to a liaison officer at the Peshmerga Ministry who handled cooperation with the coalition. Unfortunately, it would be almost a week before we could arrange a meeting at the Ministry. We were, however, finally given an appointment. Captain Kameran picked me up from the hotel, and we went together to the Peshmerga Ministry. The Ministry was in the outskirts of the eastern part of Erbil, and was as closely guarded as the Asayish headquarters.

It was a hive of activity. There were Peshmerga and many foreign soldiers milling around. I could recognize Special Forces from a distance. Special Forces don't look like supermen. They are generally athletically built and not particularly broad shouldered. They look more like marathon runners and are long limbed. They are typically between 175 and 185 cm in height. Soldiers with this body type have the best chance of getting through the eye of the needle in the merciless entrance examinations. The type who passes these tests is therefore a result of natural selection.

We were picked up and taken to an office by an officer who was Kameran's contact. Tea was served, and shortly afterwards a general came in and made himself comfortable behind the big desk. When Kameran explained why we had come, the general came over and greeted us. As he did not speak English, an interpreter translated everything. We just had time to finish our tea when it was time to leave again.

Kameran said that we had to meet a certain liaison officer, who would decide whether or not I could be admitted. As we left the general's office, a man came towards us, smiling and greeting Kameran with a laugh. He was obviously one of Kameran's friends. They spoke briefly. Then the man asked if we'd like to see the JOC-room, the Joint Operations Command. I said that I'd be more than happy to. There are only a privileged few who are given an opportunity to visit JOC in the middle of a war.

The JOC is where the war is controlled from. It is here that all the most important information comes in and goes out. It is the nerve center of the war. The JOC was full of computer monitors, maps, communications equipment, satellite links, and lots of other high-tech equipment. There were no windows, so I got the impression that the room had been specially designed and shielded.

I had been in similar rooms before, such as aboard a US warship.

There was not much light in there. And, because of the heat generated from all the equipment, the air cooling system was running at full blast. We were not allowed to stay long. They were busy, and everyone was running around on top of one another with reports of air raids, maneuvers, and everything else that was happening at the front.

We continued out of the building, across the courtyard, and into another office, where we were asked to take a seat. Shortly afterwards, the liaison officer came in, sat down behind his big desk, and asked us the reason for our visit. After Kameran had briefed him, the officer turned to address me in fluent English.

He explained that because coalition countries didn't want their nationals returning home in coffins, they had asked Peshmerga to reject any foreign volunteers. This was *not* good news. My hopes had been kept up because of Kameran's optimism about getting me in. The officer expressed his regrets, and we left the Peshmerga Ministry.

Kameran drove me back to the hotel. I was feeling dejected. Kameran noticed this and tried to comfort me by saying he was sorry.

I had had high hopes of getting into the Peshmerga. I had expected to be involved in the war, at least for six months, but perhaps for a whole year. There would have been many advantages if I was fighting specially with the Peshmerga. They were better equipped, and the infrastructure in South Kurdistan offered many benefits. Among other things, here in Kurdistan I had access to banks and the airport, so that I could take care of my private matters back home. In Syria it was the exact opposite. I could not go to a bank or use the airport to fly home to visit my family if they needed me. It was difficult and dangerous to travel to Syria, and my fate there would generally be much more uncertain. But I would not give up.

But now it was only the Kurdish militia in Syria left, with who I had already been in contact. I knew that they would be more than happy to have more professional technicians, especially those who were well educated and who had military experience, to help them maintain and repair military equipment.

Back at the hotel I called my contact in the militia in Syria. I had already said that I would join the Kurds in Rojave if I wasn't accepted by Peshmerga.

They said that I just had to drive to Sulymaniyah where I would be picked up. But first I wanted to visit Yana one last time to say goodbye.

4. The road to Sulymaniyah

My friend Hemn agreed to drive me to "Sully" (Sulymaniyah) in north-eastern Iraq. He picked me up at the hotel a few days later and we drove off.

Erbil is a circular city, built around the ancient citadel. The city has existed in this part of the Middle East since the end of the last Ice Age – a mind-boggling 9,000 years ago. Erbil is the cradle of our civilization. People were not even living in northern Europe at the time that Erbil was already a well-developed city. Researchers have shown that agriculture developed here for the first time. According to legend, the three wise men who sought baby Jesus also came from Erbil.

We drove through the small streets and came out at the ring road.

Erbil is well on track to becoming the new Dubai, not least because of its vast oil resources. The value of its oil reserves is equivalent to Denmark's gross domestic product over the next 85 years, i.e. US$ 23,000 billion. Skyscrapers have long been under construction, and investors have shown great interest. The upturn, however, was put on hold when IS attacked and came very close to Erbil. But as IS is being pushed back, daily life is again returning to normal in this part of Iraq.

Capital has invaded the city and transformed yet another region into skyscrapers, Gucci stores, and fast food restaurants.

One has to be particularly careful in the traffic of Erbil. There are no rules. That's the rule! We managed to snake our way through the south eastern part of Erbil, and fill up with petrol, water, and cigarettes. We then took the main road towards Dokan, a beautiful town near a lake in the mountains. Dokan is close to the border with Iran and is on the way to Sully.

The quickest way to Sully is to travel south, passed Kirkuk. But there is heavy fighting down there. The route was also littered with Arab guards who could be downright hostile to foreign soldiers like me. So we chose instead to travel over the mountains through Dokan, although it was a little longer. On the other hand, it was a beautiful route.

We drove off at high speed to the sound of Kurdish music, which we listened to the whole way. I was getting used to the music, but it *did* require adaptation, especially for a Westerner like me who had grown up with David Bowie and Duran Duran.

It was a scenic trip over the mountains. I had looked forward to seeing more than just the city, and I was not disappointed by the countryside. This part of Iraq is particularly lush with green fields unfolding on all sides. The mountains provided a backdrop to this picturesque scene. They were a magnificent sight. The lower parts were green, but turned brown above the tree line. The highest mountains were covered with snow. The war seemed far away in this idyllic setting. We drove southwards until the road swung east up through a pass.

We took a break on the pass and got out to enjoy the view of Iran. A long white wall of mountains runs where Iran begins. The Kurdish language also sounded more Persian and has a more melodic sound than the harsher and guttural Arab pronunciation.

At the bottom of the valley at our feet lay Dokan, which was a popular tourist destination. Iraqis would come up here all the way from Baghdad. We drove through Dokan and continued south towards Sully. Shortly after Dokan we came to another checkpoint. Unlike our previous encounters, we were stopped and asked to produce our IDs.

When the guards saw my foreign passport, we were asked to follow them into on the guard house.

Hemn was nervous because of all the military equipment I had brought with me. However, I had packed my military rucksacks into two civilian suitcases. When we walked to the guard house, a captain came out. I told Hemn to say that I was with the

Peshmerga. The guard seemed to accept this, took a brief look at my passport, smiled, shook hands with us, and let us drive on.

The winding road took us down again to the lower altitudes, and we were rapidly approaching Sully. We were still listening to the sounds of traditional Persian music; this time spiced up with techno beats, which didn't sound so bad.

I had agreed with my contact at the Kurdish militia that I should wait at the airport until I was picked up. Hemn drove to the airport's main entrance and dropped me off. He was concerned for me and asked if he should wait. I declined his kind offer, and we unloaded my stuff. I gave Hemn a hug and thanked him for his help. Hemn got back in his car and drove off.

I found a bus stop and wrote a text message to my contact, letting him know that I was ready to be picked up. A long time passed. I waited patiently, but no one came. I had dressed in civilian clothes; in cotton coat and wearing my reading glasses. I probably looked like a businessman who had just got off a plane, which was my intention. I didn't trust strangers and, only to a limited extent, my contacts; even though I had checked several sources that confirmed that they were actually who I believed they were.

After two hours of waiting, I called my Kurdish contact, who was in Germany. She apologized many times and promised to contact the man who should pick me up. I waited another hour and decided to take a taxi to a hotel. I could wait there and take advantage of the Internet until I was eventually picked up. It was easy to get a taxi at the airport, and we drove towards the centre. I asked the driver to take me to a particular hotel in the northern part of the city, where he dropped me off at the entrance.

I walked into the foyer and discovered that they were actually using their metal detector. They also had detectors in Erbil, but they never used them at my hotel. It would be interesting when they scanned my bags, because I knew they would ask me about my military gear.

Sure enough, the guard looked aghast when he scanned my suitcase and immediately called for the head of hotel security. He arrived with a friendly greeting. Weapons were nothing unusual in Iraq.

I explained that I worked for Peshmerga. The Head of Security regretted that he would have to keep the most dangerous parts of my equipment as long as I was staying at the hotel. This was not a problem, I said, as long as I got a receipt. I took my luggage and went to the lobby where they had a bar. I ordered a cup of coffee, sandwiches, and some water.

I had just finished eating and drinking when Hagi rang. Hagi, the man who was supposed to pick me up, spoke poor English, so he passed the phone to another man. This man spoke fluent English, and I was relieved to hear he had an English accent:

"It's good to hear an English voice, mate!" I said.

He was John. When I had given him my exact whereabouts, he said that they were not far away from my position. They would come and pick me up immediately.

I got ready, and shortly afterwards a Kurdish man came into the lobby. He held a phone up in his hand, walked toward me, gave me a searching look, and then looked at his phone. I had sent a photo of myself to my agent in Germany. I expect this was the image that Hagi was studying on his phone to confirm my identity.

"Jørgen?" Asked Hagi, and I nodded. I got my equipment back, and we left the hotel. Hagi had come with a taxi that was working for the guerrillas. He looked a little concerned when he tried to lift my heavy suitcase. Had I foreseen the coming hardships through the mountains, I would have known why.

We got into the taxi and drove a short distance. We then turned into a small, gloomy alley where we were dropped off outside a small house. Hagi looked anxiously around, and asked me to hurry into the building.

5. Safe House

Our safe house was about 110m². First one entered the lounge that was used as a meeting room. There were sofas along the walls, and the floor was empty. Continuing through the meeting room, one came out into a small passageway, where there was a kitchen to the left. Going straight ahead, one passed the bathroom and toilet. At the back were two bedrooms.

I threw my gear on a mattress lying on the floor of the room furthest at the back. A man came out and greeted me. He introduced himself as John. I had spoken to him on the phone shortly before. He was middle-aged, and I did not get the immediate impression that he was a born warrior. He seemed more like a nice, talkative uncle. John was a little older than me, and was formerly a "Green Jacket".

He had been in the British army for nine years and had fought a long time in Northern Ireland. John lost his best friend in an operation when they were hunting IRA terrorists. He was of medium height, with a big nose and big ears, and looked a little like one of the dwarfs from Snow White. He was slightly ugly, in a charming way. John was of Scottish descent and would later be given the Kurdish name Heval Bash – meaning Comrade Bird. He was the youngest of three siblings.

He made fun and joked the whole time. He seemed harmless enough, but it masked his true capabilities. I would later learn that he was specially trained in intelligence and knew everything there was to know about the performance and use of arms. John was therefore a great asset to our team. Later, I wondered whether John was still active in British intelligence, as he had strong inclinations in that direction. He certainly had charisma. I was sure that, in his youth, he could have talked the panties off most ladies – and probably still could!

We slept on the floor in the back room. There was a stack of mattresses and a pile of blankets one could use. I made myself a small bed in a corner and placed all my gear and my backpack beside it. I threw my suitcases in a room with several other suitcases of those foreign soldiers who had made the trip before me.

There was Internet in the house. But as power cuts were so frequent, it was almost useless. I had bought a mobile Internet connection, which I also let John use. I supported John in many ways because he had brought very limited equipment and resources with him. As I had plenty, I didn't mind sharing with him. The Kurds had suggested that we should not bring too much military equipment. Fortunately, I had ignored their advice.

The Kurds had very limited equipment, and what they had was of poor quality. Their uniforms were of a cheap Chinese make. They were not flame retardant and did not have inbuilt IR. If they were exposed to heat or flame, they would melt and burn into the skin. They didn't have any bullet proof vests. You do fight better if you feel protected by a bulletproof vest, plate and helmet.

In the kitchen of our safe house we ate directly off the tabletop. Plates were not used unless the food was liquid. We often ate *nan*, a flat bread eaten throughout the Middle East. The house was warmed by heaters that burned cheap oil, which stunk awfully if the heater was not set correctly or was not hot enough. It was unhealthy to breathe in the fumes from these heaters. We therefore slept with the windows open, even though it was winter and cold outside. We wanted to get used to sleeping outdoors. Moreover, both John and I liked to sleep with the windows open all year round as we were outdoor people.

John was a fellow mountaineer. I had hiked often in different mountains. In preparation for this mission, I had put 30 kg in weight and water bottles in my backpack. I carried it up the mountains to simulate patrolling with a pack in steep terrain, as I expected we would be fighting in the mountains frequently as well.

After two days in the house, a third member joined our group. Will was 25 years old and came from North Carolina in the southern United States. He spoke with a broad southern accent; was 192 cm tall; and had a strong and athletic build. He ate as much as three people put together, so I christened him "Cookie Monster": a character from the children's programme, Sesame Street.

Will was a very sensitive person with a strong urge to protect the weakest. He had, like John and I, been outraged by the atrocities he saw committed by the Daesh against civilians. Instead of just watching from the sidelines, he had decided to help. Will had been left homeless after his mother died. He had never known his father. Besides his military training, he was an avid hunter and had a talent for tracking (looking for traces left by animals to track them down).

Every time John made a joke, as he often did, Will giggled like a little schoolboy. It was endearing. John made fun of Will's southern accent. But Will also had a short fuse, which I could understand considering what he had been through in his short life. His father was African American and his mother was white. As he looked a little like an Arab, he was given the Kurdish name, Ahmed. This was unfortunate for Will, because he was not exactly crazy about Arabs. He found it rather annoying when Kurds asked him if he was Arab.

The days in the safe house were spent drinking tea, eating, practicing tactics, and PET: physical education and training. We also practiced various martial arts techniques. John had been boxing for many years, and I had started with Kyokushinkai at the age of six. I later changed to the Shotokan school of karate. But karate and boxing are not very useful on the battlefield.

So we focused on techniques that could kill or incapacitate the enemy. For example, we practiced strangleholds from behind and blows to the solar plexus, eyes and ears. We also rehearsed using knives to target the arteries in the groin, armpits, neck, and the knees.

In the evenings we made range cards and discussed the differences between our three countries' military. Fortunately, the US, the UK and Denmark are all members of NATO, so our training had many similarities. Indeed, they were often identical.

John was the best-trained and most experienced in terms of combat, and he was happy to share his knowledge. My opinion is that when you talk, you just repeat what you already know. On the other hand, when you listen, you learn something new. I was delighted to learn new things from John's extensive experience from Northern Ireland. I also had training in surveillance, but not as advanced as John's.

John had spent many years gathering intelligence and tracking down the IRA. He had therefore acquired invaluable experience in everything from setting up an OP to jotting down small details about the movement of vehicles or people who came and went. John also had expert knowledge about secure communications. He knew exactly which digital media were encrypted and which were not, how to communicate in code, and so on. It was this unusual knowledge, amongst others, that reinforced my suspicion that he was, or had been, in the intelligence services.

John and Will needed equipment, so we made an appointment with Haji to take us to the local bazaar. Fortunately, a country at war has an abundance of military equipment. We walked about two kilometers to the marketplace.

Here in Sulymaniyah we felt relatively safe. We wanted to synchronize the small differences in our countries' militaries when moving and maneuvering. We already started following the strategic rules for combat in built-up areas. However, we did so in an unobtrusive manner in order to avoid drawing attention to ourselves. We stopped regularly and discussed what we had just done. It would be useless to engage in urban combat in Syria without knowing each other's patterns of movement.

When we arrived at the market, John and Will started looking for body rigs. I was looking for radios of high quality for communication, something we had identified as being high up on our wish list of necessary equipment. We doubted whether the Kurds could supply us with radios. On the whole, it was hard to know what kind of equipment was available in Syria. But we did not want to miss the opportunity of acquiring what we needed, here, in well-stocked South Kurdistan in Iraq.

Will and John found the vests, warm socks, and other small things that they had been looking for. We moved back again to our safe house.

We were all wearing *shemagh* scarves and anonymous clothes in order not to stick out from the crowd. It did not appear that we attracted any attention. There were other foreigners here in Sulymaniyah, both oil workers and businessmen. And even if anyone had noticed us, it was no big deal.

We had been in the safe house for a week, and as we had nothing to keep us busy, we started looking forward to getting going and make our way to the front. Since I had also been staying in the refugee camp and been waiting for Asayish and Peshmerga in Erbil, I had now been on this mission for more than a month.

We started asking Haji about the possibility of finally getting going. He explained to us that Peshmerga had closed the border with Syria. He kept saying: "Tomorrow, my friend." But the next morning, nothing happened. And so it went on for several days. Even if the border had not been closed, the rivers were still too high for us to cross them in our vehicles. We were unsure whether Haji was just keeping us back. He spoke no English, which made it difficult to communicate.

Meanwhile, a young man in his early twenties had arrived at our safe house. His name was Ariel, and he would not survive long. We didn't know this at the time. He was too inexperienced for us to welcome him into joining our group. He was the first to attend the training camp. Ariel was from Iran and was not a Kurd.

But it was not unusual for young men without great job opportunities, or who were persecuted by their regimes, to join the Kurds. And the Kurds, being so tolerant, accepted all people, regardless of ethnicity or religion. It was this kind of reason that made me want to fight with and for them. Hence, we found

Christians, Muslims, Yazidi, Jews, Hindus, Africans, Chinese, Europeans, Persians, Arabs, Turks, and many others in our ranks.

We were brothers, and we were all equal. The Kurds had a flat organizational structure, with little hierarchy. The officers were elected by voting. Thus, it was us soldiers who decided who we trusted enough to lead us into battle. There were also many of the political leaders of the Syrian Kurdistan, which they call Rojave – meaning West – who came to the safe house. I therefore had the opportunity to meet the leadership of the organization. They made a very good impression on me. They were different from politicians in the West. They listened, and we did not get the feeling that they felt superior to us. On the contrary.

Finally, the time had come for us to leave. At least Hagi seemed more convincing this time. We packed our gear so that we were ready to man the vehicles quickly. Nobody wanted to be the one who kept the others waiting, so everything was carefully laid out and ready. Socks were put in boots and uniforms laid out in dressing order, so that we could put them on quickly. A torch was also ready, in case there was a blackout in the city, which there often was. I woke up in the night and heard some noise.

Yet another foreign soldier had arrived, who was now looking for a place to sleep.

Will had grown tired of John's complaints about his loud snoring, so he had moved into the room next door, where he also did not have to go out to smoke. Which was good, because he smoked like a chimney. I had banned smoking in the bedroom. I slept with earplugs, which was fine as we had guards and were still far from the front.

The newcomer was given Will's mattress and went to bed.

The next morning I met John on the way to the toilet and asked him who the newcomer was. John could hardly suppress his enthusiasm when he told me that the newcomer was reinforcing our troop. "He's well trained – better than us." Which said a lot. Although Green Jacket soldiers are not considered SF (Special Forces), they are generally as well trained. And with the many years of war experience that John had, there were not many SF who could teach John very much.

I gathered from John's enthusiasm that our troop had been allocated a member of the Special Forces. I looked forward to the opportunity of extracting even more knowledge for myself. I was not without experience, though. I had spent more time than most in the military.

I had participated in numerous patrols of various kinds and had fought against many Special Forces in NATO exercises. There was one particular experience with SF that I remember very clearly. During an exercise, I had caught a frogman. The frogs at that time played the role of the Fifth Column: more specifically, the elite troop Spetsnatz. Our role was to be Hunter Force.

It was the 1990s. Even though the Cold War was over by then, we still trained in accordance with blue allies vs. red enemy. That is, NATO vs. the Warsaw Pact. We used police dogs that had military training, and had chased the Spetsnatz frogman corps in GDs (Gelände wagen/ Mercedes four-wheel drive vehicles). We had caught several frogs, who had a hard time avoiding being tracked out by our dogs. Frogs were, after all, people and give off the same smell as other people.

The frogs had been separated from each other during an attack, and one of them had taken refuge on a small mound from where he had a good view. But he must have dozed off, as I was suddenly only about 20 meters away from him. I had left our vehicle and walked a few meters along a path to keep looking for the enemy. My group was only about 50 or 60 meters behind me. I had noticed something yellow, which turned out to be insulating material the frog had found on a nearby farm, which he used to keep warm. It was November, and it was bitterly cold.

When you are tired, you cannot think straight, and so you make mistakes. The frog had seen me at about the same moment that I had seen him. We were now staring into each other's eyes, waiting to see who would make the first move. The frog, who held his MP machine gun and his basis in his hands, began to run. So I chased after him. I had the advantage that I could run with nothing but my rifle. He, on the contrary, had all his gear in his hands. Yet he was incredibly fast and fit, which was not surprising. I was in reasonably good shape, but I found it difficult to catch up with him. My rifle was not exactly light compared to his little submachine gun.

But I was determined to catch this frogman and gave it everything I had. In a last gasp attempt before my strength was exhausted, I gave full throttle and reached for the gas hood on his uniform.

I got hold of him, and he surrendered upon being touched, in accordance with the rules of these exercises.

But by now we were far away from my group, who apparently was unaware that I had suddenly disappeared. I tried to call for them. I had previously experienced an SAS soldier who had tried to chin me after we'd caught him during a similar exercise a few years earlier. I knew that the frogs were also trained in close combat and was not entirely comfortable in the situation. I could neither shoot him nor use my knife. But it seemed as though he intended to follow the rules, so I ordered him towards the vehicle. He was exhausted after the long run. But shortly before we arrived at the vehicle, he had got his breath back and made an attempt to escape.

Sensing that he might try to escape, I got a tight grip on his gas hood while I walked behind him. We had a very large man in our group, who we nicknamed Brutalis. I ordered the frog down flat on the ground, put him in handcuffs, and told Brutalis to give him a "sheriff star" – pinching the nipple hard – if he misbehaved.

I went to the kitchen and greeted the newly arrived soldier. He seemed a bit stressed, which was hardly surprising. He was from the US and had a long flight behind him. Americans are particularly nervous in the Middle East, as they are of huge value to the extremists, who like to capture them, and then decapitate them on television. So the fact that Jeremiah, the newcomer, had travelled alone and unarmed to Iraq, said a lot about his courage and character.

I soon took a liking for Jeremiah, and we spent the morning talking at length about our respective backgrounds. Jeremiah was 32 years old and from South Boston, a poor and notoriously dangerous place to grow up. Jeremiah was about 180 cm tall, robust, and I would guess that he weighed around 85 to 90 kg. He was a former Green Beret in the US Army. As such, he was in excellent physical shape.

Green Berets are Special Forces that are specially trained in guerrilla tactics, intelligence, and interaction with civilians in war zones. Green Berets also learn many important languages, depending on in which region of the world the United States is involved. Arabic and Persian would be of particular value in these times, and Jeremiah spoke a bit of both Arabic and Persian.

The US Defense spends $500,000 to train each of these elite soldiers. Some young soldiers have a reckless devil-may-care attitude, and are loud and annoying. But Jeremiah was different and down to earth: which was typical of genuine Special Forces. Empty vessels make most noise. Jeremiah was anything but empty.

Jeremiah was the eldest child in his family. Without a father, he had to raise his younger siblings. It had matured him beyond his years and given him a responsible and mature outlook. Jeremiah was still very close to his brothers and sisters, something I envied him. Even though I had an elder brother we never saw each other. As his name suggested, Jeremiah had Jewish roots that went far back.

Later on we gave Jeremiah the nickname "Playboy" because he was a handsome guy and flirted with the YPJ: the Kurdish female warriors. The women appeared not to mind Jeremiah flirting with them. His friends called him: "a hippie with a gun." He had travelled around the world with a backpack. He was deeply spiritual, and when I saw a picture of his beard – nearly a meter long – I understood how he got his nickname. Like me, Jeremiah was a controversial character. I used techniques from and sought answers in peaceful Buddhism – at the same time going to war.

Jeremiah had many other talents which we would come to appreciate on our mission. One of his specialties was first aid, in which he had received long and intensive training by doctors and nurses as part of his military training. So I gave Jeremiah the first aid kit that I had brought with me, in the hope that he would be able to save lives, should one of us get injured.

Jeremiah seemed like a trustworthy character. Later on, he would become the one person in our group that I would come to trust most.

During the following days, Jeremiah and I had many interesting conversations about philosophy, history, religion and other topics. Something that particularly interested me was his upbringing in South Boston, which had also produced many well-known gangsters. Among them was the infamous James "Whitey" Bulger, who had been on the FBI's Most Wanted list for years. His capture came with a reward of two million dollars.

I was curious to hear what it had been like growing up amongst the many rough Irish and gangsters in a Chicago-like environment. I tried to lure personal stories out of Jeremiah. On the whole, I am very interested in the United States because it has so much influence on the rest of the world. Jeremiah had arrived just in time. Later that same morning Hagi told us, through an interpreter, that we should prepare for our departure.

The car came and we loaded our gear into the back. We said goodbye to Hagi and gave him a hug. The trip to the camp in the mountains took about six hours.

I had already driven the first part of the route with Hemn on the way south to Sulymaniyah. After a few hours of driving, the driver turned off the road and continued driving northwards directly towards the mountains. We stopped shortly afterwards at a restaurant by the roadside, and the driver invited us to lunch. We ate, used the toilet, and continued our trip.

      The farther north we went, the narrower and worse the roads became. Eventually we drove only on dirt tracks. We passed through several small villages on the way towards the pass. We drove up over the mountain as the sun began to set. On the other side, the decline was steep.

6. The Guerrilla Camp

All of a sudden we turned off and drove down a small dirt track towards a river. It was winter, and the water was freezing cold. The ground was covered with snow, and it was fortunate that we drove a four-wheel drive, especially now that we were off-road. I suspected that we were near the border, and that we were now on a smuggling route that would take us past the Peshmerga guards, who had closed the border with Syria. We continued driving along the river.

Then the road turned abruptly down towards the water, and we slowly crossed the river which was about half a metre deep. The road became worse and worse the further away we got from civilization and into the mountains. It was extremely muddy. The tracks went deep into the sludge; so much so that the soil often scraped against the bottom of our vehicle.

Occasionally we got stuck, and the driver had to switch to low gear to get out again. It required a lot of experience and good driving skills from the driver to move forward. We did, however, manage most obstacles without major problems. It was rare that we foreigners truly travelled off-road. One of the reasons was that few of us would put their precious vehicles at risk. We therefore enjoyed this wild ride, at least as long as we did not really get stuck in the mud.

In the meantime, it had turned dark. We had to get out and shine our torches to assess the situation. There were some large stones that we had to move before we could continue. We removed the stones and went behind the vehicle to push. After five or ten minutes of work we were finally free again and continued our trip.

Shortly afterwards, we saw a few people in guerrilla uniforms standing by the road a little further down. We had arrived at our destination.

It was obviously not yet possible to cross the border in northern Iraq, and we had to wait here in the mountains for the right opportunity. We disembarked from the vehicles, put on our backpacks, and prepared ourselves for the hike. The two partisans who picked us up wore traditional Kurdish clothes, but in a green guerrilla color. Both had Kalashnikovs.

Because of all the equipment, I was heavier than I would have liked. I promised myself that I would give away some of my stuff to others in the team. I had decided earlier that it was better to have too much than too little. I could always get rid of equipment that I didn't need, but could not necessarily get hold of equipment which I needed.

We continued to walk up towards the guerrilla camp. At first, it was hard to see where we were going in the dark. It takes about 30 to 40 minutes to build up full night vision. The heavy load didn't make it easier to balance on the narrow paths up the mountains.

After approximately half an hour's hike, we crossed a small creek and arrived at a hut.

We were asked to leave our equipment at the entrance and went inside. The hut was built of sandbags with a roof made of wooden beams and plastic sheeting. The entrance was purposely built low. You had to bend down so much that your head and eyes literally turned to the ground when you went in. It made the place easier to defend. Inside there was a burner on the floor.

Around eight to ten partisans were gathered and sat on plastic chairs around the burner inside. They all stood up and shook hands with us. There was also a foreigner amongst them. He was a young, red-haired Canadian, who seemed ecstatic to see other Westerners. It turned out that this hut was the mess, and just one out of several that were scattered around the camp. A few tables were set up and we were given food and tea.

We sat around a plastic table and were served a meal. After dinner we were assigned a hut about 75 meters away from the mess. We took our gear and went up a small hill to our new home. This hut was built in the same way, with sandbagged walls, so that it could also be used to defend our position.

Once inside, we were told to take a maximum of three blankets each to keep warm. We each found a place on the floor where we made ourselves a place to sleep. Three young guerrillas slept in the same hut as us.

The women in the camp, of which there were 10, had their own hut 50 meters south of us. Another ten male soldiers had their hut near the mess.

This camp therefore had more than sufficient capacity, at least for the moment. But it was likely that, with most partisans at the front, the numbers in the camp were at a minimum. The camp was used both as R&R (rest and recuperation), which was often needed, and as a transit base for soldiers who travelled in and out of Syria. For those who needed it, training in ideology and weapons was also provided.

The camp was well built from both a craftsmanship and a strategic perspective. This was hardly surprising given that the Kurds had been at war for decades, and had used these mountains and camps as havens for so long. A Kurdish proverb says that "the Kurds only friend is the mountains."

The Kurds have been persecuted by the regimes in Iran, Syria, Turkey and Iraq over many years. Saddam Hussein's regime had not even hesitated to use poisonous gas against the Kurdish civilian population. They wiped out an estimated 12,000 women and children in Halabja in eastern Iraq.

We were lying down and talked about the day's events. As usual, John told jokes and made fun of Will's southern accent. Will just giggled. We had become closer and were well on the way to forming a good team.

A team goes through several stages before it is forged together as a cohesive unit. These phases can be described as "formation, discord, normalization, and ready for action". I was now looking to see how this theory would apply to this team in a war situation, where there were many differences from civil life, but also many similarities. Humans are humans regardless of the circumstances. And sure enough, there was uncertainty about many things in this formation period. We were each beginning to find our place in the team. Quarrels sometimes broke out during the discordant stage that we were in.

There had been rumors that we foreigners were used only as propaganda and were spared the horrors of war and danger: something we absolutely refused to accept or come to terms with. We wanted to fight.

It could be difficult to get information out of the Kurds, since they either did not know, did not want to give us information, or were not allowed to. We were new, and they probably did not know whether they could fully trust us yet.

The young Canadian was still excited about his new company of fellow Westerners. The Kurds had given Joshua the Kurdish name "Arden", which meant fire, because of his red hair. Joshua was 20 years old, about 190 cm tall, very thin, and weighed only about 75 kg. He was pale and had Viking tattoos. He loved heavy metal and weird Norwegian sounds, which he called "Norse tunes" – and claimed was music!

Josh was mature for his age and very smart. He was the oldest of a group of siblings from Alberta in Canada. He had a formidable knowledge about Russian weapons and quickly became our "go-to" expert in the field. Josh also had a pioneer training from the Canadian military and had therefore learnt how to use explosives. Josh was still a big boy, innocent, and although he was almost an adult, both John and I, being the eldest, felt responsible for helping Josh cope and return home to his family unharmed.

We were woken up at six o'clock every morning. It was the guerrillas' camp, and we had to follow their routines. The toilet was a small tent with a hole in the ground. Toilet paper is not used in this part of the world. As I was well aware of this, I had brought a plentiful supply. But strangely enough, I very rarely needed to go to the toilet. I was not quite sure whether it was due to the new diet or because I had started smoking again. I had quit smoking for many years. But after just a few days in the safe house, where everyone smoked and there was nothing else to do, I had started smoking again.

I promised myself that I would smoke during the war, but would quit again when I returned home – if I returned home. I loved to smoke, but when my daughter was born, I realized that it was too risky. A thought popped into my head: wouldn't it be ironic if I survived the war then died of lung cancer!

In the same way, I continuously looked for karma and consequences of my actions. I knew that there were forces that we humans do not understand, but which partly control our lives. These were powers that could blow us like a feather in the wind. If we were not aware of them, we could have no influence on where we were being blown.

I went down to the mess where we had arrived the day before. As I walked, I noticed the beautiful surroundings which we had not seen the previous evening in the dark. There were mountains all around us. Although it was winter, it was relatively green. There was some snow here and there on the mountains higher up. There were many bushes and trees, and the area could be classified as semi-open. Several small brooks ran down the mountain to the south of us and formed a small stream.

The earth was warmer than the air, and there were whiffs of morning fog and mist in different places. It was magical. I felt humbled by being here in the mountains of northern Iraq.

The Zagros mountain range runs from Turkey down to the Persian Gulf, and forms the borders between Syria, Turkey, Iraq and Iran. It was formed by the Arabian tectonic plate pushing under the Asian plate, lifting these mountains higher and higher. The mountains are still rising to this day, and there can sometimes be violent earthquakes in this region. The mountains consist mainly of limestone. As limestone is made from sediments deposited over millions of years, this was a paradise for geologists.

Both John and Jeremiah were mountaineers. As such, they had a broad knowledge of mountains and what they were made of. Ignorance of the rocks they were climbing could, in the worst case scenario, mean death. John often came running excitedly, trying to rouse our interest in one new type of stone or another that he had discovered. As he was usually greeted with a yawn or a laugh, he eventually stopped trying to impress us with his rocks.

The air here was cold in the early morning, so I went into the mess to find a plastic chair near the heater. We were served tea and nan. There were various kinds of toppings I hadn't come across before. I ate virtually everything that I was served. But if I had a choice, I would rather eat something that looked appealing. "Appealing" was not the first word that came to mind when the dishes were old, dented tin bowls that I would not have offered my dog! It was probably because I had been living in civilization recently. I would just have to get used to the simple life again.

I knew it was very good for me to experience life in this way, without luxury. I had tried it before, when in the military, and not least when I had lived in Africa for a year. It was while we were working on a project in the middle of a civil war. I knew that these experiences made one more humble and more appreciative of the privileged life that we live in Europe.

I tasted some of the different dishes. There was a yellow substance that looked and tasted like marmalade. There were also thin white slices; a kind of cheese that I assumed had been made from goat's milk. Then there were olives. I quickly got used to this simple life. It would not be long before we would be eating – with our bare hands – animals that we had just shot with a pump gun, while a heap of dead bodies laid only meters away. At this point, though, I had no idea about what to expect.

After breakfast, we assembled on a little hill outside the mess. We started making range cards and discussing how we would attack the camp: how many men we'd need, and what weapons we'd use. It was normal for us to plan an attack on our own base. In this way, we could detect weaknesses in our defenses of the camp. We did not expect to be attacked; but you never knew.

We had still not been armed. Our hope was that we would be issued weapons before we crossed into Syria. In a war zone and so close to the enemy, we felt defenseless without weapons.

The camp was on a plateau. From the west to the east it was surrounded by a ring of cliffs facing northward. Any attack would undoubtedly come from the north. From there, one would have the advantage of fighting downwards against the camp. We therefore focused our range cards in a northerly direction.

When making a range card, you draw all prominent objects onto a map and estimate the distances to these. You then assign a specific group to an area that they – and only they – must defend. This helps avoid concentrating all weapons on the same place. It is the commander who gives orders about fire and combat and, in general, only he may deviate from the rules.

As we didn't have distance measuring equipment, we used another effective technique. Each team member estimates the distance to an object. The average of these estimates usually proves to be very accurate. If you want to be extra careful, or if you have to defend a position over a long time, you can go into much greater detail when preparing range cards.

We all made a range card and afterwards compared them. Then we discussed the distances to, for instance, rocks or clusters of trees. We focused on analyzing which route an enemy would opt for when approaching the camp, and how best we could prevent an attack from that particular area. The day passed with these exercises, interspersed with meals and tea breaks. In the camp, one went to sleep by about 8 o'clock.

I was suddenly awoken in the middle of the night by a loud howl...*Uhuuuuuu*. It sounded again. It was wolves that had approached our camp. I thought it was rather quaint that there were wolves here in the mountains. But then again, it was not my sheep or children that I had to worry about. The Kurds and our guards certainly did not care about wolves, which they called *gurga*.

I went back to sleep, but woke up a few hours later, while it was still dark, and needed to go out to take a piss. On my way out, I met one of the young Kurds who had been on duty who was just on his way in, and another Kurd on his way out. We greeted each other briefly, and the new guard walked to the mess. I made for the bush that I had chosen as my night piss spot. Having relieved myself, I was about to go back to the hut, when I suddenly got a strange feeling of being watched. My night vision had not yet fully adjusted, and my eyes were still blurry.

I lowered myself slowly into a kneeling position and sat still while I used my senses to scan the area. My breath made little clouds of mist in the cold night air, and I had goose bumps. Suddenly I heard an almost inaudible sound behind me. I turned my head slowly.

Behind me stood a large, grey wolf, which stared intently at me. It was so close that I could look directly into its large eyes. It reminded me of my old German shepherd, although it was much bigger.

I wasn't afraid. But still, I lowered my hand slowly and felt for my knife – just in case it should decide to attack. To always be prepared, we slept with our clothes on. So fortunately, I had the knife in my belt. But wolves rarely attack larger prey alone, unless they are desperate. The wolf had probably found our leftovers and had a night snack.

I wondered why the wolf had not run off at the sight of me. Perhaps I had surprised it. As it was ages since I last took a shower, I thought by now I had lost most of my human smell, and smelt more natural. The wind came from the direction of the wolf towards me.

We looked at each other and waited for the other's reaction. The wolf looked indifferent: neither frightened nor aggressive. I felt the same. Suddenly the wolf lowered its head, sniffed the ground a little, and ambled slowly back in a northerly direction. When I went back to the shelter, I could not sleep. I kept thinking about the wolf.

The next morning, Juggernaut came into our quarters as usual, shouting "Roj bash! roj bash! - Good morning! Wake up!" like a sergeant. We had nicknamed this Kurd "Juggernaut", as he was unusually large and a brute. He was just over 190 cm tall and broad shouldered. He had a lot of hair on his arms and face, a big, thick stock of black hair and brown eyes. Juggernaut was different from other Kurds. From his psyche, I imagined that he had had a tough childhood, was poor, and possibly an orphan. He was belligerent and generally ill-tempered.

We were a bunch of thick-skinned, rough guys who were not afraid of Juggernaut. Each time he was rude, we just teased him. Although he was bigger than us, we knew from experience that size does not mean much. Personally, I preferred bigger adversaries if there was to be a scuffle and if I had to fight. That way, I did not have to feel guilty about handing someone a good whack. Juggernaut probably sensed that he could not get the better of John, Will, Jeremiah nor me, so it was usually young Josh that he tried to bully.

But we didn't hate Juggernaut. He was more like a cartoon character. Making fun of him became a big part of our entertainment, and therefore he was welcome in our company. We joked that to defeat the Daesh we would only need to drop Juggernaut in a parachute behind enemy lines. He would flatten the lot like a rhino!

"Joch! Joch!" Juggernaut would yell. It means "No! No!" Juggernaut considered it his job to keep us in line. If he suspected anyone of having taken one blanket too many, he would be there immediately, "Joch! Joch!"

When I came out of the hut, I saw Will sitting some distance away from the living areas and looking down at the ground. Will was an avid tracker and hunter. When I went over to him, he showed me his discovery of wolf tracks in the snow. I just smiled at him without saying anything about my encounter with the wolf. We went down to the mess together where we were served breakfast.

After breakfast, Heval Rokan called us together and said it was time we were given our Kurdish names. Heval Rokan was an elder guerrilla who had lived and fought in the mountains for decades. She was respected – not only because she was one of the eldest.

She gave John the name Heval Bash (Comrade Bird), because he seemed intelligent and had a crooked nose, like a bird's beak. Will was christened "Ahmed", in keeping with his Arab looks. Josh had already been named Heval Arden (Comrade Fire), because of his red hair. Jeremiah was called "Kaharoman", which means strong. When it was my turn, I could see Rokan hesitate. She thought, and took some time before she said "Gurga" (Wolf). I looked at her astonished. This was weird! But suddenly she changed her mind and said "No! I name you 'Heval' (Comrade)." And so it was that I was christened Heval Heval (Comrade Comrade).

In the afternoon we used our time to practice maneuvers and tactical advance.

We divided ourselves into teams A and B, and planned an attack on an imaginary enemy force, which was represented by a protruding cliff. We went through the principles of advance from cover to cover, and through cover. We discussed the differences between cover to provide protection against weapons and cover that provides protection against visibility by the enemy. We also discussed the penetration force of the new type of weapons that we were expecting to be issued with.

After several of these simulated attacks, we were *in theory* equipped with different weapons and we rehearsed our movements with PKCs and precision rifles. As Will had the biggest physique, and therefore found it easiest to carry heavy weight, he was "assigned" an PKC. Although John, Kaharoman (Jeremiah) and I all had been trained in precision shooting, it was Kaharoman who was "assigned" a Dragunov (Russian sniper rifle), as he had received specialist training at the school for Special Forces. A marksman has relatively greater freedom to find an area or object from which he can provide "overwatch" (cover for own troops).

The PKC gunner also provides a form of overwatch for troops as they maneuver. The two weapons were, besides rockets, the main weapons used by our group.

During training, we suddenly heard several Kurds cheering. They told us that one more city had been liberated from Islamic State. It could only mean one thing: a barbeque and Kurdish traditional dancing to celebrate the liberation. At last, we would get protein, which we rarely got. We were served vegetable soups of various kinds virtually every day.

Later in the day, we came together on a flat area. It looked like a big lawn. The Kurds took out a ghetto blaster, formed a line and began one of their folk dances. The sun was shining, and although it had been freezing cold at night, the temperature was now more comfortable. We also wanted to experience the culture and the community, so we decided to join in the dancing.

There were several types of dance. Some of them were easy and could be learnt quickly. It was really festive and fun to join the guerrillas in circle dancing in the mountains.

In the evening we gathered outside the mess, where we barbecued chicken over the fire. We ate our dinner while enjoying the wonderful view. Then we withdrew to our shelters and prepared ourselves for bed.

I woke up again in the night. I had pushed the blankets off me and I was freezing. I sat up to find the blankets to pull them over me again. I noticed a shape bending over. It was next to the entrance near our bags. I also heard the sound of a zip opening and closing.

At first I thought that it was one of our guys looking for something in the bags, but the size of the figure was not the same as any of us. I also noticed that the bags were being opened very carefully. I decided to get up and check what was going on. When I got to the entrance where the bags were, I found a person huddled in fright, sitting completely still. It was one of the young Kurds who had his hands in our bags. I asked him what he was looking for, but he didn't answer. He just moved to the side.

I was disappointed that one of the Kurds would steal from us. I decided against telling the others about it. I would rather talk to this heval myself the next day. The young hevals were poor and only owned the clothes they were wearing, and perhaps an extra set of underwear.

I wondered if there was any point in trying to punish the young man. Instead, I tried another method, which my Buddhist Ajahn had suggested. I pulled the young heval aside and explained to him that I had seen what he had done, and that I would be keeping an eye on him. I also gave him ten dollars, as I understood that it was poverty that had made him steal, not necessarily greed. The Kurdish freedom fighters shared everything and they had a different relationship to possessions. This made it almost normal to take what one needed.

When I gave him the $10 I could feel his bad conscience radiating from him. I knew I had done the right thing. He would never forget this gesture because thieves in this part of the world usually get very rough treatment. They could even be physically punished and expelled.

The next day, a few fighters from the front arrived at the camp. A young YPJ fighter – a female guerrilla – was wounded, and her left arm hung limply. Kaharoman had noticed this too. She would now benefit from his extensive medical training. With the assistance of one of the other Kurds who understood a little English, and acted as interpreter, he asked the young warrior where it hurt. He examined her arm and quickly got a sense of what might be causing the pain.

I went out to smoke a cigarette. When I came back into the mess, Jeremiah was busy massaging her shoulders. The young woman not only had pain in the arm. She seemed also to ache in her soul. She had been at the front in Kobani a long time and suffered from both the mental and physical wounds of fighting. The young woman never smiled. All in all, she looked very sad. She was quite pretty. She had long chestnut hair and green eyes.

Many Kurds look like Westerners. This shouldn't be so surprising. They are the original Indo-Europeans, from whom many Germanic tribes originate, including Scandinavians. In this part of the world, you could find eyes of the wildest and strongest colors: from blue, green and brown to a mix of colors not seen anywhere else in the world.

The days went by, and as Kaharoman (Jeremiah) massaged the woman's arm and shoulder, she was gradually able to use it more and more.

Virtually in proportion to Kaharomans care, the spark returned in the young warrior's eyes. She even smiled occasionally. She was beautiful when she smiled. The rest of us were not sure whether she got her spirit back and smiled because her arm felt better, or because of all the attention she got from Kaharoman. But regardless, we were well-pleased with Kaharomans efforts. As we were trying to win the respect and trust of the Kurds, this support made it easier for all parties to cooperate. We laughed and teased Kaharoman, telling him that he had a good technique to get women to smile.

In the evening we talked about who in IS we hated the most. Jihadi John was at the very top of the list, along with the other foreigners and our fellow nationals. We considered them traitors to the countries in the West that had taken them and their families in, and had provided them a new life and a haven from persecution.

The days passed quickly, and we had been in the camp a long time. We started getting impatient about making our way to the front and finally give the Daesh one good thrashing. After all, that was our aim and the reason why we had given up our lives and jobs to travel here.

John and I went to the camp leader to get information about the possibility of crossing the border and the River Tigris into Syria. It had been raining a lot, and when the rivers were high, it had been impossible to get going. The captain promised us that we would be leaving very soon. We had heard this so many times before – also in Sulymaniyah – so we pressed our point a little stronger. We let him know that, although we loved their company, we had come to fight rather than enjoy ourselves in a camp. He understood that, and guaranteed us that we would soon be off to the front.

The very next day we were told to get ready. We yelled in unison "Fucking Irene!" That was the code word for "Go!" It came from an actual and famous combat action in Mogadishu, Ethiopia. I had given the young guerrillas more of my stuff, as well as donating equipment to my team. I was now a little lighter, which was good because we couldn't carry much with us over the border.

7. Tigris

We set off from the top of the mountain camp on the plateau and down into the valley. It was a steep decline. We had to tread carefully because we each carried a heavy pack. We left as darkness fell, otherwise it could prove dangerous. All movements to and from the camp had to take place at night so that its whereabouts would remain unknown. These were the rules. John took out a parachute line, which we all held to guide us down. It would have been better to have had a thicker rope, but it was all we had.

Our team now consisted of five men: John, Will, Jeremiah, Josh and I. In addition, there were four Kurdish guerrillas who had joined us on their way to the front.

I was particularly heavily loaded as there was still some 30 kg of equipment in my backpack. I was glad I had trained for several months before my departure. This training had included many long hikes in the Swiss mountains with a full pack. I was now glad that I had done this preparation.

We were to walk for many hours in the mountains and sometimes in muddy conditions. Fortunately, we reached the valley quite quickly without any incident. We continued westward, and there was now a footpath to follow. The temperature dropped rapidly after sunset here in the mountains. Our breath steamed out from our hard working lungs into the crisp, cold air.

There was not much that eluded the wolves' attention. I was wondering whether they were watching us as we slowly moved out of their territory.

After another two hours of hiking we came to a small river. A truck was waiting, ready to take us the rest of the way to the River Tigris. There we were to cross the border under cover of night. There was limited space in the vehicle, so we had to squeeze together in the back.

The Kurdish Peshmerga, who were guarding the border with Syria, were under pressure from Turkey not to let soldiers across the border. Occasionally, however, they closed their eyes to crossings. It was difficult to know when they would prevent crossings and when they would turn a blind eye.

We had been told to look as local as possible. We therefore tied our *shemagh* around our heads and tried to blend in with the other soldiers. We sat like sardines in the back of the truck. As we had to drive on small, winding mountain roads, it was not long before we all had aches and pains, and sore tailbones. But as professionals, we use techniques to divert our attention away from our discomfort.

I began to tell a few jokes to distract our thoughts. But I needn't have bothered, as we suddenly hit a bump. The others groaned in agony as their tailbones were crushed against the steel bed of the pickup truck. I couldn't help but laugh. There came another thump every two kilometers or so. Each time I laughed. And because I laughed so heartily, the others couldn't help but join in. Soon the uncomfortable journey turned out to be quite merry.

We came to another checkpoint with guards, and we were asked to lower our heads and keep quite.

Anything could happen when out in the mountains at night. It had been rumored that these soldiers had shot at people who tried to cross the border into Syria. From the bed of the truck, I could glimpse through the misted window and see our driver and the guard who had stopped us at the checkpoint.

The guard was wearing a green camouflage uniform and had his Kalashnikov at the ready. I could see his finger was on the trigger. There were a few other guards behind him. The whole area was lit by spotlights, and in the background I could see a heavy machine gun position. It was not just a checkpoint, but a small fortress. The guard spoke to our driver in Kurdish.

The driver nodded and handed him a document. The guard flipped through the document, every now and then looking skeptically at our driver. He then took a step backwards and shone a torch into the back seat of the truck. If he happened to discover us now, our journey would have been in vain. We were nervous that the guard would go behind the truck and look in the truck bed. We sat deadly quiet while he shone his light into the back seat.

He asked a passenger in the back seat a question, and seemed to get a satisfactory reply. He requested documents, looked at them, and handed them back. The guard was so thorough that I felt certain that he would also check the bed of the truck. That would be the end.

The guard glanced at the bed, and was just about to go behind the truck, when his cell phone suddenly rang. He took a few steps back and answered the call. We waited anxiously. Another guard suddenly came forward and waved us on. The car revved up and we continued on our way. We breathed a sigh of relief.

After a while, the truck turned down a small road, and we arrived at the ferry crossing. We had arrived at the River Tigris.

I had been looking forward to crossing this river for a long time.

We got out of the vehicle and put our packs on our backs. We walked a short distance down to the quayside and mingled with the other soldiers. It was crammed with troops. At least three companies had gathered to cross the river. All wore the same green camouflage.

Spirits were high, and cheerful Kurdish songs were sung. There were small women with big machine guns and men with RPG rockets. But most were carrying a Kalash as their principal weapon. In general, everyone was armed to the teeth. You could sense by the mood that the Daesh were now in for a thorough thrashing.

It was unreal to be here, crossing the Tigris from Iraq into Syria. I felt the euphoria of the many battle-ready men and women. We were heading into war and towards our destiny. There was no sense of apprehension, only joy and high morale.

There were about 500 soldiers crossing the river, which far exceeded the ferry's capacity. Luckily, the river was only about 150 meters wide. Two ferries were making the crossing, each taking about 30 to 40 soldiers at a time.

We were in no hurry to get across. We just stood there watching this impressive spectacle of eager, singing soldiers on their way to war. The women had the same uniforms as the men. But women will be women and, of course, they had flowery scarves. These were all similar in colors of black, red and blue, which matched their uniform rather well. Some even had pink shoes.

But we were well aware that one should never misjudge these women. Although they looked cute, they were warriors. They were our most feared weapon against the Daesh: not only because they were talented and fearless soldiers, but also because the Daesh firmly believed that they would go to hell if killed by a woman.

The Daesh were ignorant. Their superstition would be their downfall. It often happened that they fled when they discovered that they were fighting against women.

There were also guards at the pier. Since we had been told to try to look like locals, we had wrapped our shemags around our heads and mingled with the Kurds. A group of foreigners would be easier to spot. I stood amongst a group of Kurdish soldiers. Up close they could probably see that I was a foreigner; also by my equipment.

Our leader made sure that we came down to the ferry quickly so that we could get across before being recognized.

One of the ferries arrived and bumped into the dock. A crew member jumped ashore and moored the rope around a bollard. He held the hawser while the fighters began to board. Because I was heavily laden, it was not easy to climb aboard the ferry and keep my balance. But I eventually managed, and I promised myself to get rid of even more weight soon. But I had at least brought the equipment into Syria. There would always be a use for it at one of the bases.

One could see the force of the water as the Tigris flowed rapidly southwards. From the light of the spotlights one could occasionally discern an object in the water and get an idea of the river's speed.

There was a haze over the water, but no wind. It was a magnificent sight, which I tried to hold onto and enjoy. Although it was cool, we were sweating because we were heavily clad in our clothes and because of the weight we were carrying.

There were also some fish birds on the river. They stood on the shore under a group of trees some distance away. They did not seem to be disturbed by the commotion caused by all the soldiers. They were probably used to activity here at the quayside. This area had been inhabited for more than 10,000 years and this pier was amongst the oldest of its kind in the world. I wondered if this crossing had inspired the legend of paying the ferryman for the final journey to Hades.

Imagine: this part of the world – this cradle of civilization – had been around for 5,000 years before the pyramids were built. And the pyramids themselves were built about 5000 years ago. In no way did putting this place in historical perspective detract from the excitement of crossing the Tigris.

Water splashed up on the sides of the ferry while we chugged slowly away. About half way across we passed another ferry coming in the opposite direction. With my big, heavy military backpack, I had to hold onto the railing to steady myself as the ferry rocked.

The moon helped light up the river. Down here in the Middle East the crescent moon does not stand straight up, but has its "back" to the ground and its "horns" pointing out into space.

The river kept pulling us southwards. The helmsman had to keep the ferry facing starboard to steer us towards the wharf. At the last minute, the helmsman backed up. It jolted when we knocked gently into the pier. The crew jumped ashore and fastened the mooring. The troops on board began to disembark. Those who carried heavy weapons were assisted with their loads.

John, Will, Josh, Jeremiah and I went ashore and came together a little further away from the quay between some vehicles. They had come to pick us up. The mood was still cheerful and we hummed along to the Kurdish songs. Finally, we were in Syria. Our showdown with the Daesh had moved a step closer.

8. HQ

We boarded the vehicles that were lined up and waiting for us. When they had been loaded with soldiers, we drove westward in convoy. The locals sometimes gathered along the road, waving and cheering for us. While some had Kurdish flags, others had Kurdish militia flags. We continued driving for a while, then turned off the road and began to climb up a small mountain. The road wound up the hill until we reached a checkpoint.

Big flames were burning out of tubes in the background. I assumed that there was oil or gas production nearby. The boom was lifted, and we drove into the base. Everybody got off the vehicles, and we gathered ourselves into groups.

Apart from a foreigner who was on his way home, the five of us were the only aliens at the base. As we were a relatively rare sight, we stood out and received more attention. The women and girls giggled, and looked and smiled at us. Jeremiah got most of their attention.

Later, more foreigners would join the Kurdish militia. But at this time, there were only about 50 of us scattered throughout Rojave.

We were assigned a room in some container buildings, which would be our dorm for the night. There was an elderly Dutchman lying on one of the mattresses. He didn't make a very good impression. He spoke with a hoarse voice and was chain-smoking. He was unkempt and looked like someone who had just come home after a night on the town. He talked too much and bragged about being an elite soldier and a former intelligence officer. I decided to keep my distance from this man, not least because there was nothing to back up his claims.

The mattresses and blankets stank even worse in this place than usual, so I tried to find blankets that didn't give off a stench that was worse than dirty old underpants. Most nights, I slept soundly because of all the exercise and fresh air.

The following morning breakfast was served in the open. It was a buffet where one could help oneself to nan, cheese, jam and tea. It was simple and low-fat food, and we were all beginning to lose weight. This did not matter for most of us, with the exception of Josh, who was already very thin.

There was a stunning view of northern Rojave. From up here in the mountain we could see the Turkish border to the north. And to the south were flat green fields running down to the Iraqi border, where the peaks of the Shingal Mountains rose in the background.

We had been told that we were continuing to the Academy, which was a base where all new soldiers underwent training. Although we were experienced soldiers, we agreed to the Kurd's plan to send us to the Academy. Our aim was first and foremost to gain their trust and respect, and we were in no hurry. Once we arrived at the Academy, we could prove ourselves, and then be sent on to the front.

Besides, it was not a bad idea to have a closer look at the Russian weapons, some of which were different from the weapons that we were familiar with.

After only two days at HQ we were told that we had to get ready to move on. We were pleased, because there was not much to do at this makeshift base, where conditions were far from optimal. We packed our things once again and went out to the entrance of the base, where we were collected by a pickup truck shortly afterwards.

We had gone only a very short distance down the road, when we turned right and drove slightly up the hill in the opposite direction. We drove through several security checks and had to zigzag through a number of machine gun positions until we got to the western part of the base. The tight surveillance was an indication of the great strategic importance of this stronghold. We arrived at an administration building and were dropped off. We were then shown into the office building and led into a meeting room.

Most meeting rooms in Rojave, including this, had carpets on the floor and cushions along the walls, where you could sit and drink tea and discuss the agenda. There was already a soldier and a general in this room, and they stood up and greeted us. We sat down on the cushions and waited for a short while. A small elderly woman and her secretary came in. They went around and shook hands with us, and then took a seat opposite us. The woman, who was one of the Kurds civilian political leaders, began to talk about the war and the fight against IS.

After speaking briefly, she asked us to tell her about ourselves and why we had decided to fight with the Kurds against the Daesh. When it was my turn, I told her my age, nationality, my civilian background, and my military training. I also told her about Anas, who had been abducted by IS. The older woman just nodded and interrupted us occasionally to ask questions.

John was ambitious with regard to the role that he would like to see us play in the war. He made sure that the Kurds realized that we were experienced soldiers who were not in need of a month long stay in a training camp. John had only taken three months of his time to go to Rojave and fight, and therefore he could not waste too much time at the Academy. The rest of us had set aside much more time to be involved in the war, and therefore not in such a hurry.

But we were all limited by several factors, such as families and financial considerations. We received no pay and we could not go on fighting for years, especially those of us who also had responsibilities at home. I wanted to know more about what plans the Kurds had for us. We had all heard that we foreigners were being used for propaganda purposes. I wanted assurance that we would get the chance to fight at the front and not be parked at different bases for decoration.

I therefore asked directly whether they would let us fight at the front. The Kurdish woman explained that it was up to us whether we wanted to fight at the front or support the war effort in other ways. We were volunteers, and they would not force us into something that we were not ready for or able to do.

During our journey to Syria, I had slowly reconsidered and decided that I wanted to fight at the front and not only provide support as a technician. The other well trained soldiers on my team had given me the confidence and courage. I trusted them and I knew that we would fight for each other. We therefore had a good chance of survival.

We were served tea. After about an hour's conversation, our personal details were documented, and we were all photographed. We said goodbye, left the administration building, and boarded the vehicles again.

We drove down the mountain and continued towards the Academy while the sun set and threw an amazing red light over Rojave.

9. The Academy

After 10 minutes' drive we turned off the main road and onto a small dirt track. The driver put down his foot, throwing up dust behind the Toyota. As usual, Persian rhythms were blasting through the speakers. After having driven a short distance on the dirt road, we came to a building complex. A sentry opened the boom to the Academy, and we drove into the yard.

We jumped out and were directed to a building. Fortunately, this building was in better condition than the other base that we had just left. We quickly got a general idea of our new home and agreed to place our mattresses along one wall and our gear along the opposite wall. We were now near the front and had to behave tactically. We had to always know exactly where our clothes, boots and gear were. Everything had to be packed for departure and ready for action within minutes.

We then went into the mess, which was in an adjacent building, to greet our new hevals and instructors. Everyone was friendly and welcoming, and we were asked to take a seat at the table in the middle of the kitchen. We were served the standard evening meal, which consisted of vegetable soup, nan and tea.

We finished eating and went outside to smoke our customary "after dinner" cigarette.

It was good to finally have arrived at a permanent base in Syria. We could now try to develop closer ties with the Kurds, as well as get information about the war and the current situation. We could prepare ourselves and be at the front in short order when it came to our turn to contribute. The temperature outside was below zero. We turned up the heat in the house and pulled the blankets over our heads. That night we all went to bed contented.

The next morning I got up early. I had noticed that the toilet building also had showers and I had been looking forward to a real wash. I hadn't had a proper shower for several weeks. In the mountains we had only been able to have a cursorily wash. It didn't matter that the toilet and shower building was raw concrete without tiles, windows or doors, as long as the water was hot.

The whole base was under construction, and there were builders working everywhere. The Academy had been put up hurriedly in order to train new recruits in the southern part of the camp, and to house instructors and foreigners and have a mess in the northern part of the camp.

After my shower, I started to decorate our new home. I asked for nails and a hammer and put up a few shelves for our things. I found a rope and put up a clothesline for drying clothes. We needed routines and a feeling of having a kind of home after having travelled around Iraq and been in the mountains for so long. It had been almost two months since I first arrived in Erbil. We all needed to wash our clothes. Laundry had, of course, to be done by hand in a tub near the toilet building.

While I was washing my clothes, I thought about how hard it must have been in the old days when all work had to be done by hand. I felt grateful and humbled – once again – thinking about the rather luxurious life we lived at home.

After lunch we were summoned to a meeting with Captain Renas. Renas was approximately 40 years old and of average height for a Kurd, i.e. about 170 cm. He had a thick moustache and seemed calm and balanced. Rena seemed contented, like a person who had a mission in life. He welcomed us using a civilian interpreter. He told us that he would be our instructor for the next few days or weeks, depending on our training needs.

Renas explained the rules and routines in the camp. Then it was our time to talk. We took the opportunity to thank him for their hospitality. Having clarified that we had military experience, we said that we would appreciate learning more about Russian weapons. We said that we needed to be issued our own weapons and the opportunity to calibrate them at the shooting range.

Renas nodded and said that we would be given a training programme, and that we could then evaluate the situation after a few days. When we felt ready, and when the instructors also felt that we were ready, we could go to the front. Renas seemed trustworthy and sincere, and we were happy to have a man of his caliber as our instructor. Before we left, Renas informed us that here one woke up for physical training at five o'clock each morning.

At five o' clock the next morning Jeremiah and I were ready at the main entrance, wearing our sport outfits'. Jeremiah was Special Forces, and it took only a brief look at this man's stature to know that his body was his temple. I'm an early riser and I don't need an alarm clock to get up early.

Unfortunately I had started smoking when in Sully and was now worried about my lungs and what impact it would have on this morning's workout. The night before, John had reminded us that it was important to follow the rules of the base, and that we all turn up for training at exactly five. But John himself did not show up this morning. After a while, Will and Josh came sauntering along with sleep in their eyes.

To our surprise, the place was deserted. Apart from the guard, there was not a single Kurd in sight. We wondered if they had pulled our leg and had lured us out of our nice warm beds to drill us. We noticed the lights in the recruit's buildings go on in the southern part of the camp. Soon afterwards, young men came walking towards the main building. When we were all assembled, a sergeant arrived and sent us running around the building. The next 45 minutes were spent running and moving, followed by various stretching exercises. Jeremiah and I then finished off with our own personal training by doing some push-ups and other strength-building exercises.

Later in the morning, Renas came to our quarters. He had a civilian interpreter and a Kalashnikov with him. We gathered around Renas on the floor. Then he began to demonstrate the weapon by telling us about its properties, i.e. its weight, ammunition, range, etc. Afterwards he dismantled the weapon and explained all its internal parts and their functions.

After this demonstration, we were asked one by one to strip the gun and put it together again. When it had got boring up in the mountains, we had taken the opportunity to dismantle and reassemble Kalashnikovs blindfolded; competing with one another to see who could do this the fastest. So it was easy for us to do this exercise with Renas.

Rena then proceeded to demonstrate the three basic shooting positions: standing, kneeling and lying, which differed slightly from the techniques we used in NATO. But we said nothing. We occasionally had to bite our tongues when there was something with which we completely disagreed. Afterwards we politely explained that we had used, and were trained in, techniques that differed in certain respects.

We needed weapons to practice different techniques and we pushed to get these handed over to us. We were each provided with an ancient Kalash (Kalashnikov / AK47), a Karnas (Dragunov sniper rifle) and a PKC (Russian light machine gun). Newer weapons were desperately needed at the front, so only the old and worn out ones were used for training. Every time we received training on a new weapon, we went over the differences between what we learnt here and what we had learnt in our respective armies.

Some claim that you have two ears but only one mouth, meaning that it is more important to listen than to talk. I listened, because I didn't want to miss the opportunity of absorbing Jeremiah's invaluable Special Forces' training and knowledge. With age, many people develop an ego which stunts their further development. They stop having role models and start believing that they can no longer learn from others. Diminishing and suppressing one's ego has countless benefits. One of them is to never make oneself too proud to learn. We finished our training in the afternoon.

The next day's trainings with Dragunov sniper rifles (which Kurds called Karnas) was on the agenda. We made sure we learnt the Kurdish names, as we might need them at the front. It wouldn't do any good in the fog of war not to know the name of such things as ammunition or first aid. Jeremiah, John and I all had had training in precision shooting. But we let Renas pass on his knowledge of the subject without interruption.

The Dragunov was an older type of rifle that required its own particular knowledge and training. More modern rifles used for precision shooting could easily reach as far as 1,000 meters. But with the Dragunov, even experienced marksmen would have difficulty hitting a target from 600 to 700 meters. The Dragunov ammunition did not have the same power as more modern types of ammo, such as caliber .338 Lapua or the .300 Win Mag: not to mention the .50

caliber rifles which a marksman could shoot from 2,000 meters with precision.

The Dragunov has a special telescopic sight, which was very modern in its time; but its glass was of a poorer quality than more modern telescopic sights.

Personally, I preferred the .300 Win Mag, which had almost the same power as a .338 Lapua, but which had a little less recoil, and therefore better precision. I also trained privately with a .300 Win Mag. As the ammunition is half as expensive, there is also an economic aspect to take into account.

In the middle of the lesson, Renas took out the Dragunov, cocked it, took off the safety catch, and pulled the trigger. *BANG!* The loud crack startled us. The chamber had not been empty. Luckily, the rifle had been pointed upwards. For security reasons, rifles must always be aimed upwards or downwards when pulling the trigger. Renas blushed and apologized profusely. That's what can happen when one works with weapons

We began to train ourselves in observation. We played a game where we put a series of objects on the floor in front of us: a torch, a pack of cigarettes, a clip, and other things. We then had 30 seconds to observe as many details as possible. Afterwards, we put a towel over the objects. We then chose an object and described it in as much detail as possible: its color, size, markings, and so on.

John had operated in Northern Ireland for years, and these exercises were used to sharpen the ability to observe details. Monitoring and observation had played a big part of the war when they were tracking down the IRA (Irish Republican Army) in Belfast and elsewhere. John had a special knowledge of intelligence, and I lapped up his experience.

John was also extremely fussy about OPSEC (operational security); which was a good thing. You can't afford to make mistakes in a war against an enemy as ruthless as the Daesh. John definitely had a talent for infiltration, and he seemed determined to win the Kurds respect and trust. This could give him access to information and influence.

John detested the media. Every time there was a reporter near us at the front, he was long gone. One day a journalist took a picture of him at a distance with a zoom lens. But John had noticed it. He went straight up to the photographer and insisted that he delete the image.

At dinner time a supply truck arrived at the camp. We had asked for some chocolate and we were provided with a box. We worked and fought without charge and had several times refused payment. We had not come for the money. To fight without pay and put our lives at stake was our contribution towards the struggle for humanity. The future would show how much our services would cost us.

The chocolate had been sent to our quarters. But after our tea break we discovered that several chocolates had gone missing. Suspicions quickly turned to Will, who we had nicknamed the "Cookie Monster", after the voracious character from "Sesame Street." He was constantly hungry and demolished food galore. An investigation was launched and, sure enough, empty chocolate papers were discovered behind Will's mattress.

We agreed to teach Will a lesson, while having a little fun with him. We therefore formed a tribunal that would accuse, try, and convict Will for his "crime".

We gathered in our quarters, shaking with laughter as John recited a very long and authentic indictment against Will. Josh and Jeremiah were called to testify, and I was the judge. In the meantime, Will was covered under a blanket of shame. After the witnesses had spoken, Will was allowed to have his say and defend himself against the charges leveled against him. After several excuses and apologies he confessed to his misdeed.

I sentenced him to write above his bed, "I've been a bad boy", and to cook us two meals and make two rounds of tea for everyone. He accepted the verdict with a gracious: "All right, ok."

The following day, training with a RPG was on the programme. Renas demonstrated the rocket launcher, and we took turns learning how to operate it. The RPG7 was one weapon that was seldom used by our armies. For that reason, we had been looking forward to seeing it demonstrated.

As we had now been at the Academy for a considerable time, we were preparing to move to the front. Since we understood that everything takes time to organize in Rojave, we informed Renas well in advance that as soon as we could competently handle unfamiliar weapons, we wanted to proceed to the front.

Occasionally General Mustafa came past the Academy and greeted us. Mustafa was an elderly gentleman with grey hair. I assumed that he was in his late fifties. One could sense from his demeanor that a great responsibility rested upon him as a general. He was a calm and patient man, like most Kurds. Mustafa drove an old, worn out Toyota; not one of those big, new and impressive four-wheel drives that actually corresponded to his rank. In this way, he was also modest.

He had been present during our meeting with the leadership at the headquarters when we were asked about our motivation to fight in Syria. Mustafa had told me that he had family in Denmark. I got the impression that he kept an eye on us to see that we were being properly looked after. We had lunch with him one day at a table outside of our quarters. We explained to him that we were ready to move to the front. All we now needed was simply to be issued with weapons and calibrate them at the shooting range.

We were enjoying ourselves in the sun with a cup of tea, which you can only do in the winter in Syria. In summer it gets too hot. The war seemed remote at this moment; although we knew that the front was only a short drive away. After lunch, Mustafa had asked us if we wanted money or any other recompense for our efforts. But we had all declined his offer, and made it clear that we had not come for the money.

Our base had recently been "reinforced" with two new puppies to be trained to guard the Academy. All bases and guard posts in Rojave had dogs to help guard. We christened one puppy Titan, to give him confidence.

The Kurds often goaded the dogs, and Will thought they were sometimes too harsh with the puppies. But the Kurds intentionally made them aggressive. They were not pets, but were raised to become vicious guard dogs. If they were petted too much, they would become too friendly and useless against the Daesh.

The sunsets in Rojave were amazing. We had a great view to the west from the base and we were able to watch this inspiring and breathtaking spectacle every evening. It was winter, and because temperatures were low, there was less heat rising to create a haze that limited visibility. For the same reason, the night sky was equally impressive. Jeremiah knew a great deal about stars, and we often stood outside the main building after supper discussing the constellations and philosophizing about life in general. Venus shone brightly from her usual position, low in the western sky.

Jeremiah told us how the Green Berets used the stars to navigate, and I gave him a little hint on how the two rear wheels on the Big Dipper could be used to locate the North Star. I told Jeremiah about the time when some frogmen and I had sailed a two-mast, 85-foot sailing boat across the Western Atlantic Ocean. All we had to navigate with was a compass.

But the light of the compass had been so intense that it ruined our night vision. So when we looked ahead, we couldn't see properly. We therefore decided to turn off the compass and navigate by using the stars instead. We would pick out a star or a constellation and kept this on the starboard side of the main mast until it had moved too far across the sky, and no longer indicated north. We would then find a new star to guide us.

You stand by the rudder for hours and "dance" to the rhythm of the boat, as it undulates with the waves. You have the wind and the taste of salt water in your face while steering the vessel over the ocean on a small planet in an immense galaxy. To sail a boat across the sea, using only the stars – as sailors have done for centuries – is an almost spiritual experience.

The next day we had PKC training. The Pulemyot Kalashnikova is an excellent one-of-a-kind light machine gun. It is simple, robustly built, and almost always works without jamming if it is just cleaned, and if it is not too old or worn out. But even older PKCs often work far better than other PKCs.

Our group had agreed that Will, because of his strong physique, would carry the machine gun (PKC / "gimpy"). But after hearing news that the Daesh had crucified a child, I began to consider whether I should request a machine gun for myself as well. I would stand a better chance of annihilating more Daesh with a machine gun. Carrying a machine gun and its bands of ammo would be hard work, especially if one had to walk a lot. A little weight training would do me good. Although my weight was already on the way down, I could still lose a few more kilos.

After lunch it was finally time for shooting practice. We walked past the recruits' quarters in the southern part of the barracks on our way to the shooting range. The young men, some as young as 15 or 16 years old, were running around playing football on the large square in front of the buildings.

You quickly become an adult if you grow up in the midst of a civil war. I was very fond of these young guys. They had almost nothing, and as Kurds, they were harassed by the government. Many had lost their parents. But they were always in good spirits, with few exceptions. They would look curiously at us alien fighters.

We often practiced tactical advance in urban combat, and they would gather around and look on with interest. We moved forward and shouted commands: "MOVING" - "CLEAR" - "GOING RIGHT" - "CONTACT" - "BANG, BANG, BANG" - "I AM OUT" - "RELOAD".

Our uniforms were different and we had modern devices which they often came and examined inquisitively. I gave several of the youngsters some equipment that I could well do without: parachute cords which, although they were thin, could lift a car; bracelets that could be unwound and used as a tripwire, to hang yourself with if captured or as a clothesline, depending on needs. I also gave them T-shirts and other things. In this way, I was also able to reduce the weight of my backpack.

We continued past the recruits and came out on the fields behind the barracks where we turned right.

In Syria, many of the fields consist of red, sticky clay. It's a real bugger. As it had rained the day before, a kilo of clay had quickly stuck under each of my boot. Automatically, my "the glass is half full" mentality kicked in, and I appreciated the extra training that my leg muscles would get by having to wade through the mud. One has about 90 seconds to re evaluate any annoyances like this and turn the situation to advantage – before the brain starts to get frustrated and complain. This re-evaluation technique is one of the most indispensable mental tools available, and is referred to as "reappraisal technique" in psychology.

We arrived at the shooting range which was about 500 m southwest of the Academy. It was simple, consisting of a few sandbags and a bulls eye on a tripod about 75 meters away. The disc was manually operated by a person who hid in a small bunker to the right of the target zone. Each time we had shot, he stepped out of the bunker, went and read the target, and announced the results on the radio. This procedure required great confidence. But for someone used to being shot at by the enemy, this shooting range was child's play.

We took turns to shoot with the Kalash, the Dragunov, and the PKC. One condition that had to be fulfilled to go to the front was to pass the shooting test. We all did this with flying colors.

Limitations were put on how much ammunition we could use. We were not given permission to use much as it was badly needed at the front. I had had prejudices against Kalashnikov rifles in terms of accuracy. These proved to be completed unfounded. Kalash were as accurate as other rifles, at least at distances of up to 200 meters, which was plenty. For longer distances, we had the Dragunov and the PKC.

After shooting practice we washed and got ourselves ready for dinner. We always ate in the kitchen at the mess in the main building. The main building was also a simple construction. There were raw concrete floors, and steel doors and windows. You entered into a lobby where there were a couple of armchairs. To the left was a meeting room with cushions on the floor along the walls. Straight ahead was an office and warehouse. And to the right was the kitchen, which also served as our mess. The mess was simple, and reserved for officers and commanders. There was a large cupboard with provisions to one's left as you entered. A large fridge stood in the back corner. In the middle, a long dining table with benches on each side had room for about 14 men. Along the wall to the right was the kitchen with a gas stove and sink.

The food was simple, like at the camp at the top of the mountain, and it was served in tin bowls. It was usually rice with various types of vegetable soup, often made of onion and tomato. There was always nan. However, we Westerners had the luxury of having fruit and Pepsi delivered to our quarters.

We had more or less been through all the weapons, but we had not done hand grenade training at the camp. We had all thrown hand grenades before, so we could have done without this exercise. But, as this was part of the training programme, we politely accepted.

When we had finished our training, Renas and the other instructors were more than satisfied with our readiness. We had also taught Renas a few things along the way. Nothing now stood between us and the front, and we prepared ourselves for departure. All we needed was our own weapons from the depot.

It was about time. None of us wanted to be in Syria without our own weapon, whether or not we had guards at the bases. The following day we were picked up in a minibus.

We said goodbye to the instructors and the staff at the base, who had by now become our friends.

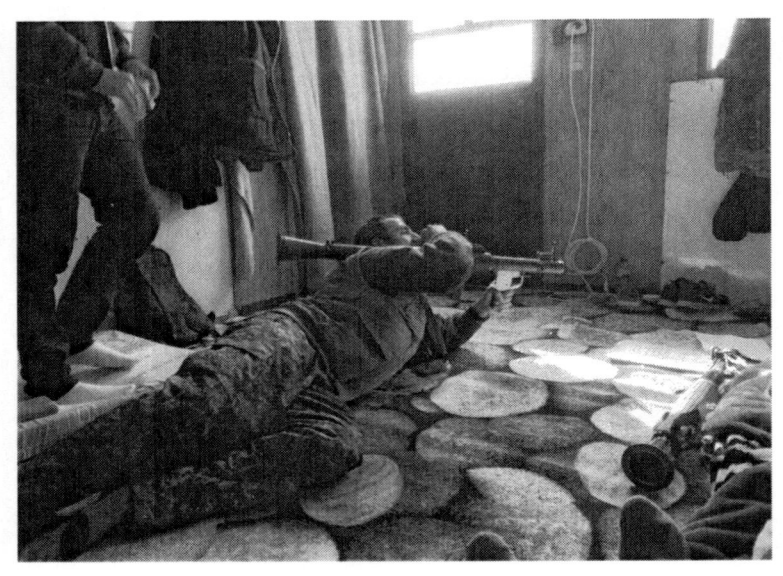

10. Serekani

It took about three hours to drive from the Academy in eastern Rojave, through Al Qamishlo, to Serekani. The town of Serekani sits on the Turkish border near the western front. The driver put his foot down. As usual, Kurdish-Persian rhythms blared through the speakers. Many of the songs were about the war, but most of them were cheerful. By now we had become accustomed to the local music. We had even found a few favorite tunes to which we sang along: much to the amusement of the Kurds. They laughed and applauded every time we sang their songs. There was great camaraderie.

Many of the towns we passed through were relatively poor. But at least there was the hustle and bustle of lively trade going on, which was a good sign. We stopped along the way to buy some food and drink for the trip. I had got out of the van to smoke a cigarette, when one of the Kurds asked me to follow him. I was in full battle gear, and people looked at us inquisitively as we went into the store.

Soldiers were no rarity, but my different uniform and equipment, and the fact that I was obviously not a Kurd, made me something of a curiosity. I was a bit nervous. I was in uniform, but beyond having a knife, I was unarmed and could hardly defend myself against any attacker with a Kalash. We bought some necessities and went back to the car.

When we arrived at Al Qamishlo, we had to make numerous small detours to avoid Assad's soldiers. Al Qamishlo was divided something like Berlin during the Cold War. The Kurds held both sides of the city up to its centre, while the Syrian government still occupied the city centre itself. But there was an agreed ceasefire in order to take on IS. Everything seemed peaceful. Moreover, most of Assad's soldiers came from the area and had little desire to fight against their Kurdish neighbors.

We arrived at the base at Serekani late in the afternoon. The female branch of the Kurdish army had their base right next to the men's. Many of our weapons were produced, stored and repaired at this base. It had previously been the headquarters of the Syrian President Assad's military forces in the area. The base was therefore well suited for the purpose.

At one end of the base were a few large garages, which were used as workshops. Next to them were a prison and a weapons depot. The personnel barracks were at the opposite end of the base.

We parked the van at the main entrance, unloaded our belongings and carried them inside. An

American came out and greeted us. His name was Joshua. He was a former Marine and had received a "Purple Heart" (a US military honor) while serving in Iraq. Americans receive a "Purple Heart" if they are wounded in combat.

We were invited into the office and, as usual, served tea. Joshua immediately began to brief us about the situation, the conditions, and the rules. He had even been given his own room. Fortunately, we were allowed to sleep there for the night. Once we were issued with our weapons from the depot, we would hopefully quickly move on to the front.

The front was only about 20 minutes drive to the south-west. From there, it was only another 50 or 60 minutes' drive to Ar Raqqa, the stronghold and headquarters of IS. That we were to fight so close to the IS stronghold, could only mean one thing: fanatical and fierce resistance from IS.

Serekani was a border town. Only a few hundred meters away from the base was the Turkish Border. It was closely guarded, with security towers every 200 meters. The border had three metre high fences with floodlights and NATO barbed wire. The Syrian part was poor and in ruins after the heavy fighting when the Daesh had been thrown out of the city. The Turkish part, on the other hand, was prosperous. It was so close by that people on the Turkish side could stand on their balconies and drink tea while the war was being played out in front of them.

We met with the local commander at the office in the main building. I handed him the document with our order, which I had received from headquarters. He read through it, muttered a little, and said, "Ok, you can stay here tonight. Tomorrow you'll be issued with your weapons and sent to the front."

As there was not much space in Joshua's room, we were squashed together. But by now we had become accustomed to this kind of discomfort.

Joshua had lots of weapons hanging on the wall. We wondered why they were not being used at the front, where they were most needed. The next morning we were handed our rifles. We were all issued new AK-47 Kalashnikovs. That is to say, they were in a new and unused condition, but had been made in the 1970s.

They had no PKC or Dragunov to spare. But we were happy to be given Kalash in such good condition. Most of those we had seen before were really old junk. We were also issued with 150 rounds of ammunition: that is, 30 rounds in five magazines. We loaded our magazines and got ourselves ready to move to the front. Soon afterwards a van came and picked us up.

We drove back towards Serekani. Inside the town we turned south along a main road. We were finally fully equipped and ready for battle. As we drove southwards towards the front, you could feel the tension in the car. Now it was for real. There was complete silence as we made our way southwards towards the front.

All was quiet before the storm.

11. The Western Front

We made our way through several small villages on the main road. After about 15 minutes, the driver turned left and we continued down a smaller dirt road for another five minutes. All the houses in this region, which looked poor, were built of clay. The driver pointed out which of the villages were backing the Daesh and those which supported the Kurds.

We eventually came to a narrow tree-lined road and continued along it until we reached some buildings. The vehicle stopped, and we all got out. We had arrived at the western front.

A group of young soldiers, both men and women, were standing outside one of the buildings. They all came over and greeted us warmly. We were then shown our living quarters. The entrance to the room was just a hole in the clay wall. The door consisted of a blanket that was hung in front of the hole. Some carpets had been laid on the ground. On top of the carpets were mattresses on which we were to sleep. There was no floor in the building. Another hole had been hammered through the opposite end of our quarters, which led into a kitchen.

It was winter, and cold. With openings at either side of the room, a draft ran through our dorm. As the whole ceiling was black with soot, it looked as if there had been a fire in the building. On the whole, it was pretty run-down. There was not the slightest comfort to it. But being at the front, you have to consider yourself fortunate if you can simply sleep under a roof in dry surroundings. We might have had to spend our nights in a muddy trench.

We were told that our new home had recently been recaptured from the Daesh. It felt a bit strange to think that we were now living in the former house of the enemy.

Having arrived at the front, we needed to improve our contingency plans and introduce a number of security procedures and healthy habits at our new post. First, we were called to a meeting with the captain in command. He was a Kurd with a name that sounded like "Gandalf". So that is what we called him. He had fought for the PKK (the Kurdish guerrillas in Turkey) before deciding to fight against the Daesh in Syria.

I quickly took a liking to Gandalf. As he had lived three years in Germany, I could converse with him in German. Gandalf had *walked* across Europe, on foot. This said a lot about what an extraordinary man he was. He was so calm and balanced that, had I not known better, I would have thought that he was a

Buddhist monk. The man was full of vigor. One thing Gandalf told us was that, normally, we were only to fire from our respective positions. But should the Daesh launch an offensive and try to take our position, every man and woman should remain at their posts and fight. It was unacceptable for anyone to panic and flee. We fully agreed with him on this. For me, it was an obvious decision. But I wondered whether the others felt quite the same way.

We were then shown around the base and, most importantly, we inspected our defenses. The entire base was approximately 300 meters long from north to south, and 200 meters wide. Since the enemy was to the south of us, most of our defenses were set up in that direction. Our other defenses protected our flanks. All positions were armed with machine guns and RPGs. In addition, we had a truck armed with a heavy Dushka machine gun which we could drive around and fire at the Daesh from different positions.

Approximately 800 meters to the north was the next Kurdish defense position. And about 600 to 700 meters to the south was another of our advanced positions.

The terrain consisted of relatively flat fields with a few hilly areas to the south. It was therefore relatively easy to monitor. But it also meant that it was difficult for us to launch an attack. We five foreigners were all of an offensive mindset. We understood the benefit of taking the initiative and leading an offensive strategy.

It was clearly an advantage to make the enemy *react*, rather than *act*. It was extremely important to make sure that the enemy weren't given much time to rest and regroup. One should try to harass the enemy as much as possible.

All positions were built using bulldozers, digging and pushing soil into embankments, which were then reinforced with sandbags. In addition, we had anti-personnel mines laid out in front of our positions, which could be triggered by remote control.

We split up and immediately began to plan an attack on our own camp, so that we could get an overview of the camp's strengths and weaknesses. Josh and I went in a northerly direction and discovered the best ex-filtration route. Although we would stand and fight, we had to know how we could retreat and fight on from a rear-guard position if, for example, the Daesh should attack us with armoured vehicles. Since the area was flat, it was not so easy to find an optimal escape route. But there were a few elevated positions a bit further back which could provide cover. That, we decided, would have to be the ultimate escape route.

We then started to assess how vulnerable our flanks were and made drawings of the entire northern part of the camp. Later we would gather to review the whole area and discuss our plans.

John and Jeremiah had dealt with the southern part of the camp in the direction of the Daesh. The Daesh also had three positions against our three positions. Starting from the south, they were called RED 2, 4 and 6. Red 2 was located approximately one kilometer to the south. Red 4, which was the nearest, was only about 600 to 700 meters to the west. And Red 6 was approximately 800 to 900 meters away in a north-westerly direction.

We had been allocated accommodation in the north of the camp. It was slightly lower than the southern part of the camp, and thus provided us with better cover. It suited us well. There was a crew of platoon size at the base: 25 men and women. The women had their own living quarters in the middle of the camp. The men stayed in rooms next to ours in the northern part of the camp. The kitchen and mess, which consisted only of an empty room with a diesel-oil stove, was also in our building – adjacent to our room. Since a hole in the wall had been knocked out from our bedroom into the kitchen, there was a constant stink of diesel coming from the oven in the kitchen and into our room. Our lungs filled with diesel fumes and particles, and we all coughed a lot.

It was freezing at night, and the guards would come into the mess to get warm every time there was a change of guard. We were also put on guard duty. My first duty was the following night from 3 am to 6 am. There are the most amazing night skies in Syria. As there was no light pollution out here in the countryside, you could literally see millions of stars. I never tired of gazing up at Orion and the Big Dipper. They would drive across the sky during my three-hour vigil. Astronomy had its origin here in the Middle East. Witnessing this amazing spectacle every night, it was little wonder that people were spiritually inspired.

I was on duty with a Kurd, whose name I couldn't pronounce. He was a little heavily set. Perhaps I should say fat, nice, and likeable. However, on his watch he soon fell fast asleep and snored. Sleeping on duty is usually regarded as an offense that is punished by a round of beatings from one's fellow soldiers. Or even demotion. But I sat only a few meters away from him and had a good view. So I let him rest awhile before waking him up.

Later in the morning, the weather turned misty and foggy. It was difficult to keep watch. You learn a lot about your senses during such vigils. You listen especially carefully when your vision is impaired. After a while you start to hear things. If you are not aware of it, your brain can quickly start playing little tricks on you. I promised myself that the Daesh would never be allowed to sneak up on us. Not on my duty, anyway.

Throughout the day shots were fired from both sides at regular intervals. I just had to get used to it. In the beginning I was startled when the powerful Dushka fired, as it made a hellish noise. But after a few days, I got used to it. Shells repeatedly flew above our heads, so that you could hear their hissing sound. It sometimes happened that they exploded around us. But we were pretty secure behind the sand bags, and I was wearing my bulletproof vest and plate.

So I felt well protected. I had already made up my mind that if I was killed, there was nothing to do about it. It was the only way to get peace of mind. If you walked around afraid of dying all the time, it would drive you mad. I have flown often in aero planes during my life. The first few times I felt a bit nervous, especially when there was heavy turbulence. But after a while I began to think that if the plane was to crash, there was nothing I could do about it. So why worry about something that I couldn't do anything about.

I had the same attitude to the war here in Rojave. I was very cautious and always made sure I was moving under cover and keeping my head down. But I didn't think much about dying, and I wasn't particularly afraid. If it happened, it happened. In this way I found peace of mind and avoided getting distressed.

Our team got together and we went through our drawings of the base. We agreed to strengthen the flanks with acoustic alarms. These were just strings connected to empty metal cans, which would make a lot of noise if the enemy happened to step into the cords at night. We would have preferred to use the detonators from hand grenades. These are also triggered if the enemy steps into the wires, and they would detonate making a very loud crack.

John and Jeremiah built sniper positions to the south of the camp. A sniper should ideally be situated in a drawn back position. It should be a place that offers good cover while being out of sight of the enemy.

The Kurds looked at us in wonder as we were preparing our positions. The Kurds were not as tall as us. We had to excavate some of the permanent posts so that Will could stand upright in them. One was on duty for many hours every day, and it was important that it was not too uncomfortable.

The next evening I was on duty with Heval Tara. She was sweet and friendly and spoke a bit of

English. I took advantage of this opportunity to get more information about the whole situation. In many ways, our current war here on the western front was very similar to trench warfare during World War I, and it was difficult to advance.

Tara told me that the Daesh had thermal sights. There were certain indications that they had them. For example, they had been able to shoot accurately at night. I felt a tightening in my gut when I heard this.

We had already started to consider how we could attack the Daesh's RED 4 position most effectively and with minimum loss. It was a delicate situation. The flat terrain demanded extra care and attention. Attacks across open fields on foot against machine gun positions are highly risky and virtually requires Special Forces. We had assumed that they had night vision sights. But thermal targeting systems were a rarity down here, and we had thought that it was unlikely that they possessed them. An attack could easily turn into a disaster if it was not carried out with the greatest precision. We had the training to do so, and the Kurds had the courage. But whether we could coordinate such an attack, and carry it out without mistakes, seemed unlikely.

Experienced soldiers know that something always goes wrong, and that one must regroup and adapt when this happens. There were too many unknowns in this equation. The Daesh also had guard dogs, and we had to assume that they had put mines in front of their positions. Tara and I discussed which options we had to attack the Daesh and how they might attack us.

We had come here to defeat the Daesh and not just to be on guard duty in a static position. In the following days, and every night, we discussed how we could attack the Daesh's positions. But every discussion ended with the same conclusion. It was not possible to attack without heavy losses.

We therefore went ahead with plan B. We had observed that vehicles were driving daily between Daesh's positions 2, 4 and 6. They were probably the vehicles that transported the commander, changed the guards, and brought supplies. In contrast to the fortified and heavily armed positions, these vehicles represented relatively easy targets. Assault was our "bread and butter", i.e. it was one of the most basic operations that we as soldiers could carry out. We did not need lengthy discussions about how such an attack should be carried out.

There were flat fields between us and Daesh 4. But towards the south-west, between RED 2 and RED 4, the terrain was more varied. As we could sneak back and forth unseen and sheltered by the terrain and darkness, it was best suited for our attack. However, it was important that we had the wind blowing towards us, so that the dogs could not catch our scent and the guards could not hear us.

We would send a light two-man "recce" patrol, which was to observe and gather information in preparation for the attack. To this end, I had a *Ghillie* (camouflage suit), and we made another ourselves, out of rags and towels. Gandalf was unsure whether he would allow such an attack. But after we had convinced him that we were well trained for this kind of operation, and quite capable of carrying out the attack successfully, he became keen on the idea. In the end, he even offered to help with the attack. With his 18 years of experience as a guerrilla, his help was more than welcome.

John and Jeremiah volunteered for the reconnaissance patrol. The very next night, before dawn, they went off. They had rid themselves of any excess weight and had only *Ghillie*, rifles with one extra magazine, binoculars and night vision binoculars, a small bottle of water, and light rubber shoes. They could therefore move quickly and escape at a sprint, should this prove necessary. Initially, we held a meeting to ensure that everyone on the base knew that we had people out on the terrain. This was to ensure that nobody fired at them in the belief that they were the Daesh. We also ensured that we had a password, which everyone was familiar with. When one was hailed with the word "Pesh", the person had to reply "merga", otherwise you would be shot on the spot.

John and Jeremiah headed south-west out of the camp. They made their way towards a depression that could provide them with cover as they edged forward. It was only about 600 or 700 meters to where we expected it would be best to establish an observation post.

They started off quickly, but then began to move forward slowly and tactically when the terrain could no longer provide cover. They made sure not to make any sudden movements. Just as quick movements stand out in the wild, so the human eye easily detects such movements. The Daesh always kept guard outside. And with their night-vision binoculars and thermal equipment, they could see people in this terrain regardless of how dark it was at night.

It was a dangerous mission. They had to crawl the last hundred meters until they reached their position, which provided a bit of cover and a view of the road between Daesh 2 and 4. There were electricity poles along the road. In the background one could glimpse a small mountain range, which defined the boundary of Rojave.

It was winter and one froze lying on the cold ground, which sucked the warmth out of your body. They could hear the guards from the Daesh talking, and sometimes see the glow of a cigarette. But they concentrated on observing the road and vehicles and getting an accurate overview of the terrain.

Their primary task was to find out how best to carry out an assault against the vehicles, and retreat unharmed. We had to do this without being hammered by heavy machine gun fire from RED 2 and 4.

I was to have been on duty in the early evening. But I had swapped my shift so that I could provide cover should they suddenly come running back under enemy fire. But I was confident that they would not be discovered, as both were extremely well trained and very experienced. At around quarter to six the day began to dawn.

The vehicles moved mainly during the day. We therefore had no choice but to attack during the daylight hours. It was relatively safe to lie quietly out at the OP. But it was risky to move in daylight. They therefore had to remain in their position all day and only return after nightfall the following evening.

Although I had been on duty during the night, I could not sleep. I was too anxious to relax. Instead, I went up to our front position and again made myself ready to provide covering fire. The day passed without anything happening, and darkness fell. They would soon be making their way back under the cover of darkness. They had now been away for 14 hours. As I had assumed that they would come back shortly after dark, I waited restlessly.

Suddenly I noticed two figures moving northwest. They were back. I breathed a sigh of relief. We gathered for a cup of evening tea, and John and Jeremiah recounted the night's observations.

We had been almost right as to where it was best to carry out the attack. However, they identified an even better position that was close to this place. This position could offer cover for six to eight men. It was also an ideal place to open fire against the enemy. They had made a small drawing, and we began to fill it in with more details from their memory. Afterwards, we all went to sleep.

The next morning we got up and started to plan our attack in detail. Two light machine guns, two Dragunov, an RPG, and three rifles were more than enough to take out two vehicles. We met with Gandalf and asked him who were their best Dragunov gunner and RPG shooter. Gandalf did not hesitate. He immediately gave us the names of two veterans with whom he had fought for a long time.

All eight men who were part of the operation then gathered in the northern part of our base. We made a copy of the area where the attack was to take place, and rehearsed the whole scenario three times. We were only satisfied when everyone knew exactly what they had to do during our movement to the OP, during the assault, and during the retreat. Overwhelming firepower was to be deployed. This was in line with our rule of thumb that, to be efficient and minimize our own losses, we should have at least three men for each enemy soldier. However, we decided to reduce this to two men per soldier, because we had the element of surprise on our side.

Fortunately, the Daesh couldn't be bothered about tactical driving, and so they didn't keep sufficient distance between their vehicles when they were delivering supplies. This meant that we could concentrate all our firepower against both vehicles simultaneously on the same spot. In order to have maximum effect, and to justify the risk involved in carrying out the attack, we decided to target and destroy at least two vehicles, as well as all their crew and supplies.

We divided ourselves into two fire teams, with four men in each. John was the most experienced, with his eight years of Green Jacket combat experience in Northern Ireland. He would lead the attack from the Alpha group. Jeremiah, who was Green Beret Special Forces, would have the command of the Bravo Group. Will and I joined John's group, and Josh went with the Bravo Group, together with Gandalf and a Kurd whose name I have forgotten.

Although I did not have much experience with a PKC machine gun, it was not too different from the Danish PKC. So I was the designated Machine gunner in the Alpha group.

The plan was to sneak up to the forward OP, divide ourselves strategically, and take up our positions. We were each to be assigned our arc of fire, wait for the vehicles, and open fire. The RPG shooter was to fire on John's command, after which everybody was to commence firing. Alpha would destroy the leading vehicle, while Bravo would finish off the rear vehicle.

After about 30 to 45 seconds of gunfire, which was more than enough to completely destroy the vehicles and personnel, John would give the order to retreat. Alpha would provide cover while Bravo withdrew to the RV point 1. Depending on the situation, we would then either carry out a tactical movement under fire, or simply retreat back to base.

The rest of the day was spent cleaning weapons, dividing ammunition, and making our equipment ready. We had a small shooting range behind the camp. I went down there to ensure that the Pixie (PKC) was properly calibrated before the attack. For the remainder of the day we made sure we were well-rested. As we were off on our mission at 04.30 am, we were relieved of guard duty and went to bed early.

We were woken up at a quarter to four. We got up and put on our equipment – this time with extra care. We met at the mess and again went through the plan and the emergency plan. One by one we recited what we had to do, thereby confirming our understanding of our orders and precautionary measures. We were then all given the opportunity to ask questions.

We were slightly delayed, but it was vitally important that everyone understood our plan and precautions. At approximately quarter to five, and back on schedule, we shook hands and wished each other good luck. We were a team of brothers who were ready to fight and, if necessary, die for each other.

We ventured out of the camp using the same route that John and Jeremiah had used when they left the base the night before. Even at this early stage, we moved in our groups, A and B. We had many years of patrol experience behind us, and moved tactically. In the dark you walk closer together than in the daylight. We covered the sides, front and rear. Slowly and surely, we moved under the cover of darkness and the hilly terrain. I had 350 rounds with me, which I had considered more than enough for the assault. But I carried no more than necessary to avoid being overloaded. As I did not have one *single* long belt of up to 350 rounds, I had made two belts with 200 cartridges in one and 150 cartridges in the other. Both belts were loaded with armor piecing ammunition. In one belt I added tracer rounds. These light up when fired, allowing you to aim better in the dark. Using tracers, however, is a double-edged sword, because it also reveals your own position. As such they have to be used with care.

    We reached the OP without being detected and took up our positions. I lay at the far left, facing south, with my PKC. Next to me was John with his Dragunov, which he had borrowed for the job. Then lay our RPG specialist with a rocket ready to be launched. The last man in the Alpha Group was Will, with a Kalash. We lay only a few meters apart.

In the Bravo Group, first was Jeremiah with his Kalash. He lay close to the Alfa Group, so that he and John could communicate effectively. Then came the PKC gunner. As he had the main weapon in the Bravo Group, he lay close to Jeremiah to take orders about when to fire. Then there was Josh with his Kalash. At the extreme end was Gandalf with his Dragunov – ready for battle.

We had all done a "jumping test" before departure to see if any metal or anything else of our equipment rattled when moving. We had secured most of our gear with tape, which we had carefully arranged in order to leave the least possible sound signature. But suddenly there was a loud noise as one of our weapons hit against a rock. Startled, we all looked around. We lay completely still and nervous. We cursed to ourselves. We hoped that neither the Daesh nor their dogs had heard the sound. Noise always seems louder when you are close to it, especially when you need to remain silent.

We had not been discovered.

The coldest time of day was in the early morning, and we were freezing. But we were too excited to notice it much. Many of us had trained for this kind of assault for years without ever having had the opportunity to making practical use of our training

– with the exception of John. Our baptism of fire was nearing. We were gripped by a mixture of excitement, joy and anxiety.

Our choice of this particular night turned out to be fortuitous. There was both clouds and wind, which obscured our presence. The distance to RED 2 was about 300 to 400 meters; and about the same to RED 4. We were nearly in the middle of the two positions with the road right in front of us. Occasionally we heard a dog barking in the distance. But otherwise everything was quiet. We could sometimes make out the figure of a guard near RED 2. John lifted the safety catch of his Dragunov. If the guard discovered us, John would shoot him in the head, which was pretty easy on this short distance. But we were not here to depose of just one guard. We were here to destroy the enemy's vehicles and supplies.

It slowly began to get light. Soon the Daesh would begin driving between their positions in their vehicles. At around half past seven the first jeep came rushing down the dirt road. They often drove fast. It was possible for us to fire on them from our base, and they knew this. But it was difficult to hit them from almost one kilometer away. They knew this, too.

We had observed supply convoys on the road every day. Sometimes they even stopped to chat with vehicles moving in the opposite direction. We were now hoping that they would either drive slower, or that they would even stop altogether. But no matter how fast they drove, they could not dodge our bullets. We were only about 200 meters from the road. This was a good distance, if not optimal. But we had at least a little coverage here, and our own survival was equally important. If we went any closer, we could be caught in the open fields between the enemy positions, and fired upon from both RED 2 and 4.

We lay in wait for the right moment when there would be vehicles driving in convoy. We knew that we had to be patient. At around nine o clock, we finally saw a truck. But it turned down a road that led away from us. We had agreed that if there were not at least two vehicles coming together during that day, we'd remain until nightfall, and then move back to our base and try again another day. However, there had almost always been a convoy during the previous days. We were hopeful that one would drive past today as well.

It was not easy to lie still for so long with nothing to do and without being able to move. So I started to build a house in my imagination, just to have something to do. At around 11 o'clock, we observed two vehicles approaching all the way from RED 6, heading south towards RED 4. They drove into RED 4.

But shortly afterwards, the truck left RED 4 and drove south past us towards RED 2. Behind the truck drove the white jeep that we had seen many times before. We all looked at each other and nodded to indicate our preparedness. I could feel the sweat running down my cheeks. I could feel my pulse pounding. In my excitement, the hair over my whole body stood on end. I suddenly felt everything in slow motion and my senses amplified.

I heard a dog barking as it ran after a car, and tried to bite the tires. There was a black bird about 50 meters to the left of me, sitting in the field. Its head had looked blurred to me before. Now my eyes could see the shape of its beak and eyes vividly.

Every second seemed to last a minute, as if the whole world stood still. Never before had I felt such intensity in such a short time. It was a spiritual experience. But I had no time to reflect on this strange but wonderful sensation.

John shouted quietly, "Ready !" Those who had not already lifted the safety catches of their weapons, did so now. The truck continued and drove directly past our position. As I was close to John, I heard him say, "Leda!" ("shoot" in Kurdish) to our RPG man. There was a cloud of white smoke behind the rocket as it flew towards the truck. Even before the rocket had reached its target, we had all opened fire. A hail of bullets hit the vehicles.

A second later, the rocket struck the truck. A pillar of fire rose up around the cab of the vehicle, followed by a massive explosion. Light travels faster than sound, so one first sees the explosive sparks fly, then hears the detonation. If the distance is further, one even has time to duck before the bullets come flying by. It takes little more than a second for a rifle bullet to travel one kilometer. The RPG shooter had hit the target spot on.

We had grilled him into aiming slightly in front of the truck as it moved forward. We had calculated the flight time of the rocket, based on a distance of 200 meters. We then compared it with the speed at which their vehicles typically travelled, which was about 60 to 70 km/hr. The truck was a relatively large target from the side, so our chance of hitting it was good. It was important to hit the leading vehicle to bring both vehicles to a stop. It would then be a simple matter of destroying static targets. Should the rocket miss its target, both PKC's would stop and finish off the leading vehicle with heavy fire.

I was already concentrating my fire at the truck. Our second PKC was attacking the rear vehicle, which could have escaped across the fields. But it didn't. Both vehicles came to a stop. We opened up with all our weapons to put down overwhelming and precise firepower. Normally I fire for about two seconds at a time. I measure this time by pronouncing a three-syllable word, such as "Ma-ri-lyn". This has to be done to avoid the barrel of the machine gun overheating and causing a malfunction. But as I knew that we only had to fire at our target for a very short time, I fired much longer volleys of 5-6 seconds. The barrel wouldn't get too hot in only 30 seconds.

It was important to fire most of the 350 rounds directly at the target. We had to ensure that we had completely destroyed it before we withdrew. We could see the bullets hitting the target. All the windows were shot through and there were small clouds of glass splinters in the air around the vehicles. The tires punctured with one bang at a time. The vehicles slumped to the ground in the hail of bullets. The truck began to burn where the rocket had hit it. A large cloud of black smoke mixed with huge flames rose into the sky. The marksmen shot at the people in the vehicles. We did not know how many there were there, but their chances of survival were virtually nil.

The enemy in the vehicles perished quickly. In total, we fired about 1,000 rounds in a very limited area within a short time. Everything in the target area was shot to pieces. A few shots struck around the vehicles, but 80 to 90 per cent hit our relatively big target. The enemy did not stand a chance. Nor was our intention to give them a chance with our overwhelming and devastating firepower.

I quickly emptied my first belt and loaded the second belt, which I had placed at the ready. It felt that more time had passed than the agreed max of 45 seconds. When I could see the last of my ammunition belt quickly being sucked through the machine gun, I looked uneasily over at John. At that same moment, he gave the order, "Cease fire!" I only had about 30 rounds left in my belt. I wanted to get out of there before the Daesh took up their positions and started firing at us.

The vehicles that remained on the road looked like wrecks that belonged in a junkyard. The front vehicle was in flames, and a column of smoke rose from the rear vehicle. Probably the many tracer bullets would soon completely burn out both vehicles.

But we could not leave our position yet. First the Bravo Group had to return to RV 1, which was about 75 meters behind us. Only then could we retreat. Within a short space of time, Bravo Group had returned to RV 1.

But it felt like an eternity. The adrenaline was pumping through my body. At any moment I expected to hear the sound of the Daesh's heavy Dushka machine-gun. *Come on, come on*, I thought anxiously. In the same second, B group was back at RV 1, and gave the signal that they were ready to cover us. We sprinted back for dear life, which it was. The adrenaline-kick made me run like Carl Lewis on hormones, despite the weight of the PKC.

When we had all returned to RV 1, we were surprised that there were still no shots from neither RED 2 or 4. We therefore hurried further down in the lee of the hill, which provided cover against both RED 2 and 4. We then heard some single shots from the Daesh, but they were firing blindly, as we were now protected by the hill. On the last stretch before reaching the base, we would again be out in the open. But if we continued further north before crossing the open fields, we would be about 800 meters from the enemy, and therefore in relative safety.

As we got farther away and less vulnerable, we began to relax. Slowly it dawned on us what we had just accomplished. We smiled and patted each other on the shoulders. When we reached the camp, we burst out in cheers. We felt high on happiness and adrenaline. We were giving each other high-fives and hugs for several minutes. We screamed to rid ourselves of the remnants of fear that still coursed through our blood.

The other soldiers at the base, who had eagerly followed at a distance, came and celebrated with us. As agreed, they had also fired at RED 2 and 4 to give us cover. It may well have been their firing that had delayed the Daesh's attempt to take up their positions and fire at us. But we did not have much time for celebration now. A reaction had to come from the Daesh, and we were therefore still on high alert.

Sure enough, the Daesh started to lay down heavy fire at us shortly afterwards. This was a good indication that our attack had damaged them and that they were fuming. But after a short while the Daesh ceased firing. They probably realized that it was just a futile waste of ammunition.

That evening we were served with meat – a rare treat – to celebrate our small victory. Afterwards we enjoyed Kurdish folk dances. It was not a *great* victory, but it boosted our morale and unity, and did the opposite to the Daesh.

A war is won through many small and large battles. We had had our baptism of fire, and our confidence grew. Although I had felt tense and anxious, I had discovered that this had not negatively affected my fighting efforts. Adrenaline even had a positive effect on my senses.

It was only after we had returned back to the camp that I could feel both my legs and hands shaking slightly. We had survived our first real act of war and were involved in battle for real.

In the coming days our mood was excellent. We slowly fell back into our daily routine. We had received information that our soldiers, who had defeated and freed Kobane during the previous months, were partly available to support us. They would start an offensive and try to push the Daesh eastwards towards our positions.

We therefore began preparations for this battle. To strengthen our positions, bulldozers came to work at night. This meant that we spent more time out in the fields (in front of our positions) to allow the bulldozers to work in safety while building larger ramparts around our base. We had many long, cold nights ahead. When this work was finished, we started to move a large grain store, which was inside the base. These grain sacks weighed 80 kg, and there were many hundreds of them to be moved. So the following week was pure strength training that guaranteed back pain. When our preparations were complete, we went back to our dreary everyday routine.

There was some firing from both sides. There were even a few episodes of grenades striking the base. But apart from a few shrapnel wounds in the arms and legs, no one was badly injured. We sometimes had a go at the Daesh with our Dragunov and Dushka.

Otherwise the following weeks were uneventful.

When I heard that an offensive battle was underway in Shingal, I began to play with the idea of moving on to join the fierce fighting. It just was not like me to sit on my bum and do guard duty for months on end. I had come to fight the Daesh. I also had limited time. I would be financially ruined after about 5 or 6 months of unpaid time spent at the front. I had lots of bills and regular payments to make back home.

The Shingal mountains and Shingal city was where the world had watched the Daesh attack the Kurdish Yazidi civilian population. The media had shown women and children being lifted on board helicopters and evacuated away from the Daesh's brutal assault, rape and mass murder. It was, in part, these powerful images that had influenced several of us Westerners to sign up voluntarily in the fight against the Daesh.

When we were due for a few days leave in a villa a little away from the front, where you could have a hot bath, I took the opportunity to talk to Gandalf about a transfer to Shingal. He promised that he would speak to his boss about it. The Kurds looked at me in disbelief when I told them about my wish to go to Shingal. It was like asking for a transfer to the Eastern Front during World War II: a place that everyone wanted to escape from. But the Kurds respected my decision. I could feel that they admired my courage.

My own team was not so excited about my decision. But I was convinced that our front would remain static, and that nothing much would happen here in the near future. It was an opinion they did not share. But later I was to be proven right.

We parted company soon afterwards, and I was on my way back to Serekani. From there I would proceed to the Academy, where I would pick up some gear and wash my clothes. I would then proceed to headquarters and receive new orders and papers, sending me to my new unit.

12. Return to the Front

I met up with Joshua at the base in Serekani. Joshua had come back to look for a bank and pay bills. This was not possible in Syria, as the only Western Union in Al Qamishlo had closed down ages ago. To find a bank one had to travel to Iraq.

Since the last time I was there, another American, Richard, had arrived. Richard had been in Syria for a long time, and had decided to go to Iraq to join the Kurdish militia there. He gave no specific reason for this, and I didn't ask him why. He didn't owe me an explanation. It was convenient that all three of us were heading east at the same time, as we could request a vehicle together. There were also two Kurds who were going in the same direction. The next morning we travelled east. I was looking forward to seeing Renas and the others at the Academy again.

I also desperately needed a proper bath and to wash my clothes. But first I had to go to the headquarters in the mountains. I needed to be issued with new orders and travel papers for the front. In the meantime, Richard and Joshua were to arrange transport to Iraq.

At the headquarters, I met a few other foreigners who had fought at Shingal and Tel Hamees. I took the opportunity to get a sitrep from the front. A Canadian told me that an Australian soldier called Ashley had been killed when he had been shot in the head by a sniper. It was sad news, and it was the first time that I had heard that one of us foreigners had been killed. It highlighted the dangers and the severity of the whole situation.

The Canadian explained that Ashley and his team had been surrounded by a large number of Daesh when their vehicle broke down. Ashley, who was a well-trained soldier, had realized that they had to fight their way to a cluster of buildings and seek protection behind the houses. They could not remain with the vehicle in the open ground. A fierce battle had ensued as they advanced towards the buildings. It was then that Ashley had been killed.

I also met an American called Matt, who had just come back from the hospital. He had fought in Shingal, where he had been shot in the leg by a bullet going through a wall.

I quickly got my orders and was ready to get going to Tel Hamees, where the spring offensive had just started. I didn't care whether I was in Shingal or Tel Hamees, as long as it was warfare where we took the initiative and went on the offensive. I asked permission to go down to the Academy to take a bath and wash my uniform. I knew that once I was at the front, weeks could go by before I was given the next opportunity to do either.

Later that day I got a lift to the Academy. I said goodbye to Josh and Richard.

At the Academy I met Renas, who was surprised to see me. We gave each other a big hug, and I told him about the fighting on the western front. Renas was delighted that we had done so well. We agreed to meet for dinner that night so that he could hear the whole story.

Since I was last at the Academy, another eight foreign soldiers had arrived at the base. One of them was from the Princess of Wales' Royal Regiment. It soon turned out that this soldier had gone AWOL from his regiment in Cyprus and was now wanted by the British. Since the Kurds did not want to upset their British allies, he was quickly sent home to Britain. The next day we read all about this young British soldier online in "The Sun" which, as usual, wrote a lot of untruths about the whole situation.

The newcomers were very keen to hear about my experience at the front, which I gladly shared with them. I was also asked to help train a few of the new recruits, who had had no experience at all. I agreed to give a few lessons in the basic use of the Kalash. I didn't consider the newcomers unworthy, but I was soon tired of their many questions about the front. I was not comfortable always being the center of attention and looked up to as a veteran.

Although most of these new recruits had not had any combat experience, I could derecognize few good soldiers among them. But, amongst this group was also a soldier named Dan, who would soon be given the nickname "Gomer Pyle". Private Gomer Pyle was made infamous in the film "Full Metal Jacket". He was a clumsy, slow-witted character who, after being mistreated by the sergeant and his comrades, went berserk with a rifle.

It was the others in this group who had made me aware of Dan. Dan had been sitting in a corner with a sinister smile and made "shooting noises" while he caressed small cartridges. He also had conversations with some imaginary person. Dan had what looked like withdrawal symptoms, like for example the way he ate ravenously around the clock. Getting eye contact with him was impossible.

With his constant talking with this imaginary person (or persons), I surmised that Dan was schizophrenic. Another veteran in the group had come to a similar conclusion.

However, I had more empathy with Dan than several other members of this group. They harbored a mixture of fear and mistrust of Dan. It was hard to blame them. Automatic weapons and mental instability is a lethal cocktail. On top of this came the psychological pressure of war. At one time we agreed to remove the firing pin from his weapon. I couldn't understand why Dan had not been required to remain at the Academy longer. New soldiers are first sent to the Academy to be assessed. Only after being appraised are they supposed to be provided with a loaded weapon and sent to the front.

I managed to wash my clothes and myself, and after a few days at the Academy I was ready for departure back to the front. I was picked up and taken to the headquarters where I would try to get a PKC machine gun. A young and friendly Kurd at the weapons depot was easily persuaded to hand over a PKC. He even let me into the "shop". There were a couple of used PKCs leaning against the wall. After a brief inspection, I chose one that looked like it had a newish barrel. I also asked for 400 rounds of armor piecing ammunition and 100 rounds of tracer bullets, which he gave me.

I was just about to leave when I noticed a box of hand grenades on a shelf. I pulled out a pack of cigarettes and offered one to the young man, which he gladly accepted. We went outside and smoked, and I told him what a great job he was doing keeping the entire shop running. I asked if he could give me a couple of grenades. You normally get two; but he gave me four. The grenades would later turn out to be extremely useful.

I was ready for the front. Soon afterwards a truck came fully loaded with ammunition, which was also headed for the front.

In this ammunition transport vehicle, I shared a ride with an American called Perry. He was on his way back to the main base at the front, at Tel Hamees. He wanted to look for his equipment that he had left behind in haste. It was Perry who had brought Ashley's body back to the base and who had arranged to have it sent to Australia. Ashley's only family was his sister, who would collect his coffin back home in Australia.

On our left were the Shingal mountains. Shingal city lay at the foot of the mountain range on the Iraqi side. The Daesh had not only killed the civilian population. They had also raped and sold women and children as slaves. Some of the children who had been raped had later become pregnant. It was atrocities like these that made us so determined to fight for justice on behalf of these innocent victims.

Our truck was stopped at checkpoints at regular intervals. We were now in an area where there could be Daesh, even amongst the civilian population. In the back of our Toyota pickup truck lay crates of ammunition. The axles of the truck were nearly on the ground because of the heavy grenades.

We took a break en route to eat. I had taken the opportunity to buy a carton of chocolate cakes, as I found it hard to maintain my weight. We rarely got meat and we burned calories galore. In a war zone there's no need to watch your weight. On the contrary, it was important to eat as much as possible whenever possible, because your diet was so low in calories.

From the base, the drive to Tel Hamish took about two hours.

We continued west towards Tel Hamish. The mood in the car was somber. Ashley had been Perry's best friend, and they had fought together for a long time in Shingal. There had been intense battles in a built-up area, with many dead and wounded on both sides. The Daesh had artillery and mortars, and all those who had fought together in Shingal – and nearly died – had developed close bonds.

I understood that Perry couldn't fully comprehend that Ashley was gone. I knew that feeling of losing comrades only too well. But it had started to dawn on him that he would never see Ashley again. I could see and feel his pain when he talked about their plans to become police officers together in California when the war was over.

I began to think of the neural connections in the brain. Every time we laugh or cry with another human being, new neural connections are created in the brain. In Buddhism it is said that when you laugh along with another person, the other person becomes a part of you. When someone dies, these compounds are still there. Therefore, our dead friends still appear alive inside us. It takes a long time for these neural connections to gradually fade away. For Perry, Ashley would never disappear.

The huge red sun set directly in front of us as we were driving towards western Rojave. It looked as if it was setting in the road we were driving on. We were literally driving directly into the sun's last rays before darkness fell. I thought of dark omens, which made me uneasy.

The front at Tel Hamish was right there in front of us, below the sunset.

We were not very familiar with this part of Rojave. As we were close to the enemy, any wrong turn could be dangerous, and we often had to ask for directions. Once in a while we encountered supply vehicles coming in the opposite direction. Some of them carried the injured. I was wondering if I would soon be amongst one of the wounded – or even the dead.

We continued driving with the Shingal Mountain on our port side, when we finally reached the point where the road once again turned north towards Qamishlo. We were now fairly close to our destination, south of Tel Hamish.

Just as we were about to turn north, a Toyota pickup came towards us with a heavy Dushka machine gun mounted on the back. The boy who stood on the back of the truck and operated the machine gun could not have been more than 15 years old. To my surprise, he was African. I had never before seen Africans in Syria. I wondered how this boy had made his way to Syria, and how he had come to operate this machine gun.

We continued north and passed through a series of ghost towns. The towns had recently been abandoned and the shops were still full of goods. You could just help yourself to what you wanted. However, I already had enough to carry around. My only interest was in water, ammunition, and chocolate cakes – which I'd already tanked up on. It was surreal to drive through these eerily quiet dooms-day towns.

We continued northwards in the dark spring evening. We kept looking out at the fields, trying to see the battalion we were about to join. We found it slightly into the fields, on the eastern side of the road, about three kilometers south of Tel Hamish. We could see lots of vehicles from a distance, including lorries, heavy artillery, armoured vehicles and pickup trucks.

When we arrived, there was still bombardment from our artillery inside Tel Hamish against the Daesh. One could hear the loud explosions when the big howitzer guns fired at the enemy. The battalion soldiers were making a fire and preparing dinner. These were the men and women I would fight, laugh and cry within the time to come. Perry began searching for his equipment in the different vehicles. In the meantime, we backed our truck up on a large lorry which was used as a mobile depot.

We began to unload the ammunition we had brought and move it over onto the truck. The large grenades were heavy and had to be lifted carefully. We had also brought lots of crates of ammunition for small arms.

When we had finished unloading, we went over to the fire, where other soldiers had gathered for dinner. I greeted all the soldiers, who welcomed us. Occasionally, a large howitzer would fire, but it seemed as though everyone had got used to the noise. A large plate with lamb meat was passed around. We squatted and chewed on the bones, holding them in our hands. In the middle of our big circle a large fire burned.

Whilst we sat on the ground in the primitive glow of the flames, with the stars twinkling over the fields, I thought that this experience might well have occurred thousands of years ago.

After dinner the captain came over and asked me to follow him. We got into a car and drove a few kilometers back south. We arrived at a settlement where 5 or 6 Toyotas were parked. Here there was also a fire, and a bunch of young soldiers were having their supper. They approached us inquisitively, and greeted us. They looked with interest at my PKC, on which I had mounted my telescopic sights. For them, this was a novelty. I was given a cup of tea and chatted a little with the young Kurds, some of whom spoke a little English. These younger, inexperienced soldiers were kept somewhat in the background. They were used to protect the rear of our army, where it was less dangerous. As they became more experienced in combat, and grew more mature, they advanced up towards the tip of the spear, and took part in attacks.

I was assigned a hut that I had to share with 10 to 12 other young hevals. The next morning I got up early as usual – at the crack of dawn. I went outside and gathered firewood. Some young girls who had been on duty had gathered around the fire place. Together we quickly got the fire going and boiled a kettle of water for tea.

It was cold, and we all sat with our hands stretched out towards the flames for warmth. The young women were not accustomed to foreigners. One had learned a little English in school and tried eagerly to communicate with me. The others giggled when we sometimes lacked words and used gestures and facial expressions instead to communicate. I enjoyed amusing them and making them laugh, so I intentionally made funny faces. One of the girls had a laughing fit and couldn't stop. We had a very merry morning.

I wanted to reset the telescopic sight on Pixie. I therefore went to a field at the back and made a makeshift shooting range. I informed the person in charge that I was going to shoot, and began to set the telescopic sight on the PKC. The machine gun shot a little low at first, but after some time I managed to get the Pixie to shoot accurately again.

Later we had breakfast. Shortly afterwards a vehicle came to pick me up. In the background I could hear the artillery beginning to fire at Tel Hamees.

I assumed there would soon be an attack.

13. The Battle of Tel Hamees

Our spring offensive was aggressive, and I was looking forward to joining in the battle. We drove north, and after a few kilometers we arrived back at our battalion, which was getting ready to attack. There were about 15 old armoured vehicles of different types on the main road. They included several Russian T-55 tanks, a few Humvee, various armoured personnel carriers of Russian make, and a number of other vehicles that were difficult to identify.

My driver introduced me to the platoon commander who asked me to follow him. He walked quickly ahead in between some houses. We continued across an open space toward a Toyota that had a Dushka on the back. As I was carrying more than 40 kg of weapons, ammunition, water, supplies and other equipment, I had difficulty keeping up with his fast pace.

I threw my backpack in the back of the truck, and we drove off. I had arrived just as the attack was about to be launched. After a short drive, we arrived at the small suburb of Tel Hamees.

The battle was already in progress and there had been intense firing from both sides. It was only 600 to 700 meters to the center of Tel Hamees, which is a big town of great significance in Rojave. It has many residents and a large university.

The Dushka-gunner on the back of our Toyota had started firing into the city. Occasionally I could hear the now familiar sound of enemy shells flying close by us. I didn't want to remain in the back of the truck. It was a bad position to fight from. The vehicle was shaking too much for me to be able to hit anything, and it gave me no protection. On the contrary, one towered on the back and made an easy target

As soon as the Toyota stopped, I jumped out and found a more suitable position to fight from: one that was lower and gave better cover. We had arrived at the boundary of the small suburb. Between us and Tel Hamees lay flat fields where some horses were grazing. Although they seemed a bit unnerved by the shooting, they stayed in the field. Sometimes they ran for a short distance, then stopped again, and continued grazing. I wished they'd run away.

A long clay wall ran along the building where we had stopped. We started making holes in the wall to shoot through. But I knew that this wall didn't offer enough protection. So I found a few more cement blocks to put under my Pixie's barrel. My American friend, Matt, had been shot through just such a clay wall. On the western front, we had tested the local building materials by shooting at them to see what protection they provided. I therefore knew that this type of cement block could easily stop enemy bullets – at least those from lighter weapons such as a Kalash or Dragunov.

The Kurds were firing into the city. But even with my telescopic sights, I couldn't see the enemy. So I just watched through my binoculars, waiting to spot the enemy or find an identifiable target. Anything else would be a waste of precious ammunition. The other companies had moved into town from the east with the support of armoured vehicles. Our objective was to out-flank and surround the Daesh.

I was lying and watching the western part of the city, when I suddenly saw a vehicle on the outskirts of the town. The vehicle was about 600 meters away: right on the border where I could hit it effectively. I opened fire, but it was hard to see whether I had hit it. It continued moving.

Suddenly, several of our larger armoured vehicles came driving forward to our position. Their massive diesel engines were noisy; belching out clouds of smoke when they revved up. The Daesh had apparently started fleeing the city towards the west. Now, suddenly, there were even more vehicles arriving, driving at high speed out of the city, westwards. The heavy machine guns on our armoured vehicles opened fire. They hit one of Daesh's vehicles, which veered off the road. Smoke rose up from the demolished vehicle.

We also had a truck with an anti-aircraft battery on the back, which consisted of two heavy machine guns. It proved highly effective when it opened fire. A hail of heavy shells flew from the battery, followed by sticks of flames from its muzzle. I was glad it wasn't me sitting in a Daesh vehicle.

The whole day fighter planes from the coalition forces flew in the skies above us. They relayed information to us about the enemy's position. When they found a target, they attacked it. One of the fighter planes was attacking the fleeing convoy and strafing their vehicles. It roared as it came in low and opened fire on the enemy. Unfortunately, the vehicles that had tried to escape were already some distance from Tel Hamees, so we couldn't see the effect of the plane's attacks now.

We would, however, have ample opportunity to do so later.

After a few hours of fighting, the shooting subsided and we got a much needed break. We made a cup of tea and reloaded our weapons. I went into the building from which we had been fighting to look for a rag to clean my weapon. The residents had left town a short time ago in a hurry, leaving behind most of their belongings.

On the western front, we had taken over the Daesh's deserted base. But now I was in a civilian's house. It felt strange to stand in those pitiable people's homes. I went into a room where toys were lying on the floor. There was a teddy bear and a schoolbag, and I was wondering how old the children were who had lived here. I wondered how it must feel for them having to flee their homes for such an uncertain future. It's hard to witness the suffering of children, especially for a father.

I rushed outside. I couldn't stand being in the house anymore. I went over to another building that looked like a garage, and hoped to find some old rags there. But when I opened the door, the first thing I saw was a girl's small red bike. I quickly closed the door again. With a lump in my throat I returned to my tabur.

There were still Daesh inside the town, and we continued our attack. In the afternoon we managed to drive the last Daesh out towards the north-west of the town by using our heavy artillery. We began to move across the fields towards the town with cover from the armoured vehicles.

We entered the outskirts of the southern part of Tel Hamees without encountering further resistance.

The Daesh had either been defeated or had left this section of town. We moved cautiously into town. After about 800 meters, we arrived at the university.

The university consisted of many buildings in a complex surrounded by gardens with fountains and palm trees. One could imagine the idyll that would have prevailed here when the gardens were full of young, hopeful students in the dawn of adulthood.

There was a damaged Humvee, which the Daesh had left behind: suggesting that they had been based here at the university. We therefore had to be especially careful when we cleared the buildings. Daesh could still be hiding in them, and they had probably mined the university.

On the same day we were about to launch the attack on the town, I met Heval Rosa, a young woman of only 17 or18 years. Rosa was a fellow Pixie-gunner, which was a bit strange, since she was rather petite and very young. And she was wearing pink tennis shoes. But she had already proved herself in battle, and I was convinced that she was a brave warrior. As we were both PKC-gunners, we had something in common. She had also commented on my telescopic sights and had examined them closely.

Rosa had long brown hair and stunning brown eyes. She smiled and laughed a lot, and was very charming. Rosa and I took turns moving forward, doing "overwatch", thus ensuring the safe advance of our tabur.

Another soldier in our group was Heval Kobani. Together, Rosa, Kobani and I had to now move into the university and start clearing the buildings.

I swapped weapons with a younger heval who was securing the rear of the group. His Kalash was lighter and better suited for clearing buildings. The rest of our tabur went simultaneously into two adjacent buildings. The university was huge, so we had to split up in order to clear the entire building without taking too much time. While we were doing this, we could hear gunfire from inside some of the buildings further away – giving our adrenaline rush a surge.

Clearing a building is the kind of operation that requires special training. The enclosed space not only amplifies the noise from weapons considerably: the pressure from the denotation of a gun being fired increases enormously. Luckily, Rosa spoke a little English. I asked her to translate to Kobani that they should open their mouths slightly whenever they fired in an enclosed space. Otherwise the pressure inside their head could become so large that it could cause serious damage. If you open your mouth, it releases this pressure.

I asked them to follow me. I explained that I would use hand grenades should there be any Daesh in the building. The firing indicated that there were. I ordered Rosa and Kobani to cover the front so that we covered all angles inside the room. The foyer was empty and we went inside the building. Although the sun was shining brightly outside, it was dark inside. The architects had designed it to not let in much sunlight. This was to ensure a cool environment to study in.

In the next room there was a lot of empty packaging with food scraps on the floor. I felt some of the leftovers. They still seemed fresh. In the middle of the floor was an ashtray. We stared at each other when we noticed smoke rising from one of the butts. Fuck! It was only minutes ago that Daesh had left the building – if they had left at all!

I started having thoughts about masked men with large knives decapitating people. I made sure that the split pin in the hand grenade was ready to be pulled quickly. I also ensured, for the third time, that my Kalash had a round in the chamber and was ready to fire. I had never used this particular Kalash. I began to worry about whether it had been properly cleaned, if the magazines were in order, or if they might get jammed in the middle of a shootout. I had to push these thoughts aside and focus.

We were startled when we suddenly heard a sound coming from the room next door. It was footsteps. There was someone there. I held my finger to my lips and made a low *shhh...* sound to Rosa and Kobani. They both looked alarmed and wide-eyed at the door to the adjoining room. Suddenly, the barrel of a weapon appeared in the doorway. I aimed my Kalash and prepared to shoot through the wall at where the person holding the weapon might be standing. We could see the big black shadow of the person reflected on the opposite wall.

I tightened my finger on the trigger. My heart was pounding. All my senses were directed at the doorway and the person behind the wall. Just as I was about to fire, we heard a voice speaking in Kurdish. It was soldiers from our tabur. They had approached from the other side, coming towards us.

We breathed a sigh of relief. Rosa shouted something in Kurdish in a mixture of joy and excitement. The soldier just shrugged his shoulders. I don't think he quite understood how close he had come to being killed. It was literally just a few millimeters on the trigger that had separated him from life and death.

Before we continued clearing the building, we agreed with the others in the group that we should make a soft "click" sound with our tongue if we were in doubt whether it was a friend or a Daesh foe that we met in the building. It scared me to think that I had come so close to killing one of our own. It would've been a disaster if I had killed a heval. I would never have got over it. But reflecting on it, perhaps it was a good lesson in vigilance.

We continued further into the building. I thought about the smoking ashtray and whether there were still Daesh in the building. Occasionally we could still hear shots from the northern part of the university. It wouldn't surprise me if the fanatical Daesh had hidden an entire team of soldiers inside the university, ready to kill us in a suicide attack.

We moved down a staircase that led down into the basement. Now it was really getting dark. But I wouldn't turn on the lights. Instead we took a break, so that our eyes could adjust to the darkness. When we were able to see better, we continued moving quietly and carefully forward in the basement. There was some water on the floor, and occasionally a rat ran past. But it was the larger kind of rat we were looking for.

We came to another room, and I looked carefully into it. It was empty. None of us liked being here in the dark basement. But it had to be cleared. If we did not clear the basement, we wouldn't rest peacefully afterwards. If there were Daesh down here, it would be a Trojan horse. They could sneak up on us while we rested, and kill us in our sleep.

We crept stealthily down the basement hallway. The walls threw the sound around us. The slightest noise made an echo throughout the basement. It was humid and damp. Water was dripping from the ceiling. At times it was nearly completely dark.

In order not to trigger mines, I used a long grass stalk that I had found outside to sweep across the floor. If a trip-wire connected to a mine had been set, the grass stalk would locate it. The Daesh loved mines and used them continuously in all conceivable ways. They had been able to perfect these methods over the last 14 years in their fight against the Americans during the Iraq war. Both we and the Americans had suffered huge losses in this way.

We heard a sound coming from a room further down the corridor. All our senses sharpened and pointed in the direction of the sound. We made our way slowly towards the room. I had brought my rifle up to my shoulder, aiming it at the entrance. Kobani secured our rear while Rosa also aimed at the room. I had pulled her a little off to the side so that she could shoot past me.

We heard the noise again. It made a metallic sound. My heart was beating fast and the hairs on my body stood on end. We came to the door of the room. I lifted the rifle up so it wouldn't stick out in front of the door for the enemy to see. I stuck my head forward, looked quickly inside, and pulled it back immediately. It was so dark in there, I couldn't see anything.

I briefly considered tossing a grenade in there. Instead, we waited and listened quietly. The sound repeated itself again and again. It was therefore unlikely that it came from a person. The sound of a human would have been more varied.

I made hand signals to Rosa and Kobani that we should all move in on the count of three. I counted with my fingers in front of them. One, two, *three*! We rushed into the room, securing all angles. I turned on my torch. The room was empty except for a few old tables and chairs. Up in one corner of the wall was a small ventilation grate, flapping in the wind and making the sound we had heard. We sighed with relief.

We had finished clearing the basement and walked upstairs to the ground floor. In the north-east part of the university, we came to a room that looked like the sacking of Jerusalem. It was filled with desks, chairs, racks, bags, clothes and books. Everything had just been thrown around, making a thorough mess. It looked as though they had been looking for something in a panic, and then beat a hasty retreat.

We stepped extra carefully in this room as it was difficult to see if there were any hidden mines amongst all the mess. I stressed to Rosa and Kobani that they shouldn't touch anything before we had a mine clearer to scan the room. In the corner opposite us were a lot of containers on the floor. As we took a closer look, we realized that there blue wires sticking out of the containers. It was an IED (improvised explosive device), bombs and grenades.

We were standing in the middle of a bomb factory. I immediately looked at the floor to see what we were standing on. We had already noticed a whole bag of "pressure plates". A pressure plate is the trigger for a mine. If you step on a pressure plate, an electric circuit is connected, which triggers the detonator and explodes the bomb. I couldn't come to any other conclusion: there had to be pressure plates in or on the floor which would trigger the mines. And there was not just one, but about 20 large bombs in here. If one was released, the rest would go off, and most of the university would be blown to smithereens. The explosion would have been visible and audible throughout central Rojave.

"Don't move!" I shouted to the others.

"Go slowly back, the same way we came in."

"Rosa! Tell Kobani that he should go out exactly the same way he came in."

We backed slowly out of the room again, the same way that we had come in. I trembled as I carefully left the room. From the expression on both Rosa's and Kobani's faces, they were equally as anxious as me. When we were eventually out of the "bomb factory", we put up a string with a warning sign.

We had had enough excitement for one day. We were tired and needed a break. We found a heval with a radio, reported on our findings, and commissioned a mine clearing. We then informed the captain that we were taking a break, went outside, and smoked cigarettes.

A third tabur had started clearing the university from the west. After another 30 minutes, the area was reported as having been cleared. We could relax and finally get some dinner. We were accommodated in an administrative building next to the university.

There were also a few other foreigners, and I took the opportunity to get to know them. These included a large Greek named Greg. He was also a PKC gunner and, as usual, my telescopic sights on the machine gun quickly turned out to be a conversation piece. Greg had been a soldier in the Greek army. When he was dissatisfied with the level of training, he had applied to the Foreign Legion, where he spent five years.

Greg was a giant of a man with a big black beard. He was not the only legionary I had met in Syria, but he was in a class of his own. He was almost two meters tall, and his physique was almost godlike. It was not shaped like a bodybuilder, but more like a swimmer or athlete. This gave him physical strength, as well as suppleness and speed. I envied Greg when he threw his PKC and 500 rounds of ammunition on his back as if it were made of foam rubber. I, with my 80 kg, had significantly more equipment per body weight to carry around.

Greg was different in the nicest way. Although he was so big and rough, he had a gentle mind, almost like a child. He was nearly always in a good mood, friendly and outgoing. As I was talking to Greg, we were suddenly interrupted. A Kurd asked us to follow him.

We walked across the courtyard to a building where a group of civilians had gathered. The media had just arrived to film a lot of equipment in crates that the

Daesh had left behind. They asked me to examine the crates and let them know what the equipment was.

It was also new to me. But after examining the manuals and reading the instructions, it was clear that this was very costly electronic communication equipment made by a US military manufacturer.

I had thus far avoided the press as much as possible. I quickly put on a hat and sunglasses before the reporters came to film us. There were often journalists present and the Kurds continuously encouraged us to speak as much as possible with the press as part of their propaganda campaign. So, having tried to hide my identity for the last few months, I eventually agreed to speak to the media.

The press asked questions, and we responded as best we could. Afterwards we went back to our dwellings and prepared dinner. In the evening, a bonfire was lit in the yard and we danced Kurdish folk dances to celebrate the liberation of Tel Hamees. It was merry, and spirits were high.

We had defeated the Daesh and freed a large central town in Rojave.

14. The Hunt for Daesh

Within a few days, the rest of Tel Hamees had been *completely* cleared of the Daesh. The IS army had fled to the west, and we prepared ourselves to take up the pursuit.

In the morning, we broke up from Tel Hamish and joined a long convoy consisting of many different kinds of vehicles, including Humvee (an American armoured vehicle), APCs (Armoured Personnel Carriers), and other armoured vehicles. There were several large lorries with huge trailers that transported Russian T-55 tanks. About 50 to 60 Toyota Hilux four-wheel drives where also in the column, and a few howitzers. Many military vehicles were filled with troops who sat inside or hung onto them. Given the limited space in the vehicles, many troops were on foot walking along the road.

I worried about mines, which the Daesh often placed under and along the roads. I hoped they had not had time to plant them in their hasty retreat. I was in the back of a truck, lying partly over the roof of a Toyota Hilux, operating a light machine gun, which was aimed in the direction we were travelling. I was ready to provide support fire for the infantry.

Black-clad Special Forces soldiers were standing on the footboards on either side of the Toyotas, holding onto the handles of the railing. One of them was my good young friend, who I called Peter, because his Kurdish name sounded like Peter. One could recognize SF (Special Forces) by their black camouflage uniforms. They were extremely well trained. Just listening to the ordeals they had to endure in the mountains in order to be selected for SF sounded incredible.

They had to climb the mountains for weeks on end, jump into freezing water again and again, and then move on until they got warm and dry. I have previously participated in NATO exercises with both frogs and SAS, and wondered whether these guys would have been able to handle the same ordeal? Many of the Kurds have, after all, grown up without any kind of luxury and are used to being cold, hungry, and tired. And they have been at war for decades. Not many can match the Kurds resilience and mental strength.

The SFs on the sides of the Toyota were ready to jump off as soon as there was contact with the enemy. This happened daily. In the villages where the Daesh were hiding, the SFs were prepared to rapidly storm the buildings.

It was cool, but the sun was shining, and the dew disappeared quickly. I was still wearing my desert camouflage, which I had been wearing day and night for nearly 14 days now, with only a change of underwear. I had a woolen vest and long underwear underneath. Now that the sun was coming up, the temperature would rise quickly. I would soon have to take them off.

It was early spring, and not long ago it had snowed. But here in the Middle East, the climate is extreme. Although there had been frost at night, the temperature soon rose to over 20 degrees in the sun.

As we were in regular contact with the enemy now, I wore a bulletproof vest. I also put on a bulletproof plate in front, which could withstand up to six shots from a Kalashnikov (7.62x39 mm rounds). In addition, I had hand grenades and other equipment like a knife, a multi-tool, and water. All this equipment mounted on my upper body was not just heavy, but also very hot. But, because of the protection it provided, it was worth carrying this extra weight. I had promised myself that neither laziness nor discomfort would be the cause of my death. My muscles and fitness were strengthened with this extra weight. I had, by this time, lost nearly 10 kg from dragging around the PKC

(Pixie) and wearing a combat vest – and because of the low-fat diet.

The landscape was still lush and green here in the north of Syria. But only a few kilometers to the south, the landscape became barren and dusty, and gradually turned to desert. The fields were flat and cultivated. It could have been anywhere in Jutland, had it not been for the dilapidated houses and clay ruins.

Having moved forward slowly and tactically for hours, checking the road for mines on the way, it was now time for a lunch break. We had sent reconnaissance vehicles in all directions in search of Daesh. As we occupied higher positions during our advance, we planted the Kurdish militia flag high up so that other units could see that these heights had been secured. It was on one such height that we stopped for a break.

We had passed through many deserted ghost-towns. In the shops we had helped ourselves to pastries and other goodies that could sweeten the rough life at the front. We were on one of these heights enjoying the rays of the sun. In this brief moment, if you closed your eyes and forgot about the war, life as a soldier in Syria was actually quite okay. Greg sat behind me. I was very fond of his company, and I wished we could have been in the same tabur.

Our area of operation was large, and I gradually met fewer and fewer other foreigners, which I didn't mind. My Kurdish vocabulary was limited, to say the least. So I preferred not to say too much; just communicating using sign language. The relationship you develop with people you spend a lot of time with without speaking much is interesting. There are many advantages if you only make polite gestures, smile and nod. At least you don't get into arguments.

A Humvee came dashing up the hill where we were having our rest. A man with a long, thick beard got out of the car. It was rare to see a Kurdish warrior with a beard. He had a bandanna and wide guerilla pants instead of the usual digital green camouflage uniform that the Kurdish militia wear. He had a Glock 19 handgun in his vest and held a M16 in his hand. More than anything, he looked like a pirate.

As he moved forward between the troops, everybody stood up in respect and shook his hand. I realized that this was no ordinary heval who had just arrived at our camp. To my surprise, he came directly up to me and said in fluent English, "You look like a real soldier, you come with me." I looked at Peter, confused. He recognized my questioning look and said in broken English: "That's Soran, our top soldier. Go with him. He's very good."

I followed Soran back to the Humvee, but I insisted on taking all my gear with me. I'd had had bad experiences with scattering my things in different vehicles. I threw my backpack in the back. I took my Pixie and ammunition with me up into the machine gun turret. Now that I was a machine gunner, I assumed that was my place.

I had never been in an American Humvee before. But since I have had civilian technical mechanical training, it was fairly easy to quickly familiarize myself with the tower and its functions. I found a good stable position for Pixie in a place where a .50" heavy machine gun had previously been mounted. I started to rotate the tower. As we drove off, I made sure that Pixie was always aimed at and covered positions ahead of us: i.e. from where one might expect to encounter the enemy. From down below in the Humvee, Soran looked up at me and nodded approvingly.

There were a couple of cartons of cigarettes, boxes of cake, chocolate, water, and arms and ammunition on the seats of the Humvee. There was also a Kalash, so I asked for it as a "back up" weapon in the tower. I would need it should I run out of ammo, or if Pixie's barrel got too hot and began to malfunction.

Soran handed me a Chinese Kalash and said, "Here, my friend." He was nice, as Kurds tend to be.

I looked disconcertingly at the Kalash when I noticed that it was not made by one of the two Russian manufacturers which produce the original Kalash, but a cheap Chinese imitation. I put it next to the hatch behind me.

We proceeded rapidly as I scanned the terrain for Daesh. Suddenly a report came through the crackling radio. The Daesh were to the south of us where they had fired on our troops. I could sense the tension in Soran and suspected that he was looking forward to soon confronting the enemy. We continued to head south. But then new reports came over the radio, and we turned around and drove in a southeasterly direction.

We stopped on a height with other vehicles, including several vehicles mounted with 23mm Dushka machine-guns. Suddenly we heard the familiar sound of bullets hissing around our ears. This is usually the first thing you hear when making contact with the enemy. The Dushka returned fire from where the shots had come, which were some buildings about 300 meters ahead of us. Soran shouted at me, ordering me to open fire. As I had not yet been designated a target, I was in principle opposed to shooting blind. I didn't know, for example, whether the Daesh were using civilians as shields. But since the commander of the vehicle had ordered me to shoot, I fired off a few rounds. But, because I could not see any Daesh, I deliberately aimed low in front of the buildings.

We quickly headed towards the buildings, even though we did not know the enemy's strength. Soran was Soran, and for him the tactic was simple: "Attack! Kill!" However, there were no Daesh when we arrived at the buildings, but there were some civilians hiding behind them. I felt relieved that I hadn't fired directly at the buildings, and that no one was hurt.

We made a short stop to reassure the locals. After they had calmed down, they pointed east. That was all we needed to know. The chase continued in that direction. We had not gone very far before we discovered two of our vehicles north of some mud huts. They both had bullet holes in them. Suddenly our car door opened, and a wounded heval got in the Humvee. He was obviously in pain and held his hands to his back. I tried to pinpoint where and how badly he was hurt. I didn't understand much of what he said, and could see no blood.

With the wounded aboard, we drove back to the settlement we had come from. I helped the wounded man out of the vehicle and laid him on the ground. I pulled out my dagger and was about to cut up his clothes and give him first aid, when another heval came running up, saying that others would now take care of him.

I jumped back into the Humvee, and we drove back the short distance to where the damaged vehicles had been stopped by the enemy. I could feel my blood pulsing faster through my body, as it had when we attacked the vehicles on the western front. My senses sharpened, and I was ready to fight.

At that moment we were fired upon from the buildings, and I could hear the bullets whistling over my head. I thought that the relatively high tower on our vehicle would attract a lot of enemy fire. Sure enough: although Soran kept the Humvee in motion to minimize chances of being hit, the enemy bullets struck the metal of the tower. It sounded like giant hailstone falling on a window.

I crossed my fingers, hoping they did not have RPG, whose rocket could easily penetrate the relatively light armor of a Humvee. I knew that the best way to prevent the enemy from hitting us was to keep firing at him – not giving him a chance to take aim.

I fired at the building where I could see movement and the muzzle of a gun. At the same time, Soran drove towards the buildings. Pixie makes a racket when fired, so I couldn't hear what he was shouting.

Suddenly I saw three people ran behind the houses, heading south towards the Shingal mountains. I shouted and pointed to Soran. He sped after them. They ran along some long depressions in the terrain. Occasionally they turned around to fire at us. One of the bullets hit the inside of the tower, ricocheted off the metal, and smashed into the armoured glass, which shattered from the inside.

Whew... that was close. I knew that if we didn't get them quickly, they would get us. They seemed to be experienced fighters. They moved, shot, and performed like veterans. Damn it, I had to change the ammo belt on Pixie in the heat of battle, just when we were in close contact with the enemy. There was no time for that.

The last of the three Daesh was only 40 or 50 meters away from us. I pulled out the Kalash and tried to get him in my sights. But the Humvee was shaking so much on the uneven ground, and I couldn't aim properly. "STOP!" I yelled to Soran. He stopped. I took a deep breath, aimed, and pulled the trigger. The Daesh-soldier fell to the ground. I was relieved to have neutralized that danger. It was either him or us. The other two Daesh were hiding in a ditch about 50 meters further along, from where they fired at us. With their good cover, they had the advantage. The Humvee loomed up on the flat field towards them.

Bullets hit the tower of the Humvee. Soran got going again, and I couldn't aim straight. Fortunately, the brain "gears up" in such stressful situations. Although it was many years since I had last thrown a hand grenade when in the defense forces, I took out a grenade – almost without thinking – and tried to hurl it into the ditch where the Daesh were. The grenade landed about 10 meters short of them. I shouted to Soran to drive closer. When we were only about 25 meters from them, I threw another grenade, ducked, and waited for it to detonate.

A long time passed. Too long. The grenade had malfunctioned. Cheap Chinese shit, I thought, and yelled to the passenger below to pass me his pineapple grenade. But he had already pulled the pin of his grenade and was just about to throw it out of the side window. But the Humvee window was too narrow to throw it very far. He pulled back his arm to hand the grenade to me, shouting that he had already pulled the pin out!

Now, it was only the handle of the grenade that separated us from certain death. Gently, with trembling hands, he handed it up to me. Normally, I would have hesitated. But I was no longer entirely myself. The situation demanded me to be cold, calculating, and effective. At this vital moment – I was.

I established the Daesh position with my eyes; then threw the grenade down at them in the trench. It exploded almost instantly and flung one of the Daesh, who had been lying about a metre from where the grenade landed, half a metre to the side. He was dead. The second Daesh was badly wounded by the grenade, but was still moving.

I was handed another pineapple grenade, which I threw at him. It exploded. The two Daesh didn't move. But some of our soldiers, who were behind us, fired some more shots at them – just to be on the safe side. One of these hevals obviously felt a great hatred for IS. He went up to one of the dead Daesh, and with his rifle butt he hit his skull till it burst open, splattering white brain matter on the grass.

I went back to the Humvee, but Soran said that we had to bury the bodies. If we let them lie in the sun, he said, they would spread disease. I didn't want to look at those we'd killed, and certainly not touch them. But nevertheless, we threw the bodies up on the Humvee. There was limited space on the back because of the equipment, so one of the dead was thrown onto the hood. But, when we started driving, the body began to slide off. So I had to sit on the roof with a leg on either side of the body.

We drove a few kilometers back to the place where the rest of the battalion waited, and threw the dead to the ground. Other soldiers came up to the Humvee when they saw the bodies. They rejoiced over our victory and the dead Daesh. They were, after all, our enemies, and it is only human to be elated when one kills one's mortal enemies. Soran, the soldier in the front seat (whose name I have forgotten), and I gave each other hugs and rejoiced in our small victory. Other hevals came over and congratulated us. We were almost celebrated as heroes.

But I didn't feel like a hero. They had fired at us before we had even spotted them. We had just defended ourselves and nearly perished in the battle.

Later on, an excavator arrived. It made a hole and we dumped the bodies in it. Afterwards, we lit a fire and sat in a circle and sang Kurdish folk songs. I found a couple of soft cushions in one of the houses, and lay down to gaze into the flames of the fire. Looking closely into the fire, I could see the green and blue colors of the gases from the burning wood. The flames threw our shadows onto the wall of the house behind us. It looked almost as if the black figures danced on the wall.

I had killed another human being. I had known that there was a possibility that I might have to kill somebody in this war, and had wondered how I would react. I had heard many stories of veterans who subsequently had difficulty processing their killings. We grew up in a culture where killing was considered the ultimate sin. I had crossed the boundary and taken human lives. But I "digested" it quickly, and was satisfied. Had it been anyone other than Daesh, I would have been more remorseful and sorry.

The Daesh were not humans in our eyes. They had stopped being humans when they committed such heinous crimes against humanity as genocide, rape, slavery and torture. They chose to be inhumane, and we felt justified to fight and kill them. Not least, to stop them attacking the civilian population.

15. Kemal

The battalion met strong resistance in a town near the Iraqi border. Our tabur had to clear and secure the surrounding villages, as well as secure our battalion's flanks, before we launched a massive attack against the town.

We knew there were IS followers and fighters amongst the civilian population, especially in this area close to Iraq. We therefore had to be especially careful when we searched the houses for weapons. At the same time, many of the residents were neither for nor against IS. We had to behave courteously to ensure that we won this part of the population's support and sympathy. Otherwise we would run the risk that they would change their allegiance to the enemy's side.

It could be dangerous to spend the night near the Arabs' houses. They had caches of weapons in the fields nearby. On previous occasions, they had dug up their weapons and attacked at night while our soldiers were asleep.

We approached the buildings in teams, and covered each other while we went from house to house carrying out our searches. Often, it was enough for us to talk to and observe the inhabitants to know whether they were for or against us or the Daesh.

In the south of this village were two slightly isolated houses on the edge of town. The residents had left these houses, which in itself was a sign. On the walls inside we found suspicious drawings of bloody swords and Arabic inscriptions. I had also found a *nunchaku*: a martial arts weapon which consists of two sticks joined by a chain or rope. Under normal circumstances it would have seemed harmless. But in this context it indicated young men with an interest in martial arts or violence.

Along with the drawings of the bloody sword on the wall, it suggested the need to search more thoroughly for other weapons. In the living room we found a cupboard that was locked with a padlock. I forced open the lock with my rifle butt. In it were pictures of a soldier in uniform, syringes and needles, and black IS flags. Bingo! We had found the smoking gun. I asked our captain to announce our findings over the radio, so that the police could take over the investigation, and let us get on with our job.

Just as we were about to leave the house, a small motorbike with two Arabs approached the back of the building. They didn't see us until they were quite close. They seemed surprised. Judging by the expression on their faces, they weren't too happy to see us. They looked nervous.

The captain sensed it too, and primed his weapon. Both men were wearing traditional Arab garb. Being in their late twenties, and having narrow faces with big beards, they fitted the typical image of Daesh or Daesh supporters. I too primed my Kalash and lifted it up to my shoulder, but without aiming it directly at them. We could be wrong. Maybe they were just ordinary civilians. Everybody was nervous in these times. But I sensed that something was not quite right about these two men.

I began to scan them with my eyes, looking for scars and wounds that could be signs of previous fights. I also looked at their footwear and for bulges in their clothes that could reveal concealed weapons. I was reading their facial expression and body language. Before a person attacks, the muscles in their face tighten and their body tenses slightly. The eyebrows are lowered and the face takes on a determined look.

Their eyes flickered and they looked nervously sideways. It seemed as though they were trying to look indifferent to our presence at their house. But, to me, they appeared anything but indifferent. When the captain asked them to switch off the engine, I pulled slightly behind them and away from the captain so that we both could shoot without hitting each other, and such that they would first have to turn around to attack me.

The driver of the motorbike moved his hand up to the key. But at the last instant he suddenly revved up and sped directly towards the captain, who jumped aside to dodge the bike. I automatically went into a kneeling shooting position and had the motorbike in my sights. The bike was fast, so I only had a brief moment to consider whether to shoot or not. I hadn't seen any weapons. The two men could also just be petty criminals or have some other reason for not wanting to talk to us.

I hesitated. I found it hard this time to just shoot them in the back. Instead, I lowered the barrel, aimed at the motorbike, and fired. But the bike zoomed off. The next moment it had swerved behind a building. I no longer had them in my sights. There was a cloud of dust behind the bike, as they made their quick getaway. I ran out into the field away from the building to catch them in my sights.

When my vision was clear again, I saw one of our white Toyotas come rushing towards the motorbike. Inside, behind the wheel, sat a heval who I recognized from our tabur. He was one of those few Kurds who was very large and slightly overweight. His face was set like a raging bull as he chased down the motorbike. He leaned forward against the steering wheel, intent on running down the fleeing escapees. But the bike made a sharp turn and dodged his first attempt to hit them.

The motorbike had turned round and was coming straight towards me. I was now out in the open field without any cover. I had two choices. The safest option was to run back and look for cover behind the buildings. The other was to shoot and stop the motorbike. But if I failed, they could run me down – or even kill me. I went down again to the kneeling firing position and opened fire. I didn't hit them with the first couple of shots. But the next struck the motorcycle and ricocheted.

The bike was now only a few metres from me. So I got up, ready to sprint. But at that moment the front wheel of the bike hit a ditch, and lurched forward. The rider lost control and both he and the passenger flew off the motorbike. The bike landed a short distance away. The driver and his passenger groaned after landing with a thump on the ground, and having the air knocked out of them.

I chuckled to myself. It did look rather comical. Several hevals came running up, and the two suspects were now surrounded by six soldiers with their rifles pointing at them. A wrong move on their part, and they would be shot. The captain was furious. He gave the driver a sharp slap in the face, cursing him in Kurdish and Arabic. We searched the two and found a small amount of heroin and hash.

Whether the two men were Daesh, I would never find out. But if it was their house we had searched, much indicated that they were Daesh. We put the two in handcuffs and threw them in the back of the Toyota, after which they were taken for interrogation.

The Kurds didn't exactly treat Daesh with kid gloves, but they treated them far better than the Daesh treated the Kurds they captured. It was important for us to maintain the moral high ground to show that we were superior to the enemy. When you know, deep down, that you are fighting for a noble cause, it is easier to fight and easier to maintain your moral standards. If you start to become as cruel or behave as ruthlessly as the IS, it can be hard to see the difference between yourself and them. Eventually, you may even forget what you are actually fighting for.

I sometimes thought about my life after the war. I knew that it was important to return with a good conscience as part of my luggage. We all carry a story about ourselves deep within us. It is our actions that make us who we are. If we behave contrary to our inner moral compass for some time, we eventually come to despise ourselves. It is therefore extremely important that the inner voice that whispers your "story" to you, about who you are, can tell a story that you can bear to hear. You cannot turn off this voice. You have to live with it forever.

We finished securing and clearing the village. I went over to our vehicle to retrieve a pair of binoculars so that I could see better what was happening in the town to the south, where the Daesh were providing stiff resistance. Occasionally we saw massive explosions north of the town. It seemed as though the Daesh were deploying both RPGs and artillery.

Our armoured vehicles tried to invade the town, but they were met with such heavy fire during their first attack, that they had to retreat. The second wave of attacks had now been launched, and I stood and watched an armoured vehicle through my binoculars. Suddenly I saw a huge explosion near the vehicle. It did not appear that it had actually been hit, and it drove off. But later in the day we got the devastating news that Heval Kemal, alias Konstandinos Erik Scurfield, who'd been in the vehicle, had been killed by shrapnel.

I assumed that it was this explosion that I had observed that had killed him. Earlier that same morning I had sat with Kemal, eating chocolate cakes for breakfast with him. He was such a nice and likeable guy, and I had enjoyed his company. Kemal was from the British Royal Marine Regiment and was an accomplished and highly respected soldier. He was the second foreigner to have been killed within the last few days.

After several attempts to take the town, we had pulled back and called in air support. There was no reason to lose soldiers needlessly. A prudent tactic was to call in the planes first, and only continue the attack when the Daesh had been crippled by bombs from airstrikes.

Later that day two aircraft began swarming in the skies above us. I took out my binoculars and tried to identify what type they were. They flew fast, so it was not easy to recognise them at their high altitude in the bright sun. But soon both planes swooped down to attack targets southwest of the town. Through my binoculars I spotted a vehicle that tried to escape the aircraft's fire. The planes dived and fired at the vehicle. The distinctive sound of a rotating 30mm Gatling gun identified the planes. Now that they were flying lower, I could see the shape of the two A-10 Warthog Thunderbolts. *Brrrrrrrt... brrrrrrrt* went their guns.

It was an impressive sight. I was glad it wasn't me who was sitting in the fleeing vehicle. They attacked at very low altitude. As soon as they had dropped their load of bombs and bullets, they climbed rapidly, and turned side on to reduce the area of their aircraft visible to enemy fire. We followed the attacks with great excitement and cheered when we saw the smoke rising from the destroyed enemy vehicles.

The aircrafts circled and attacked several times. Every time they dived, there was a roar from the engines, followed by the distinctive *brrrrrrrt, brrrrrrrt* of their guns. It was an experience I'll never forget. When the planes had discharged their load, they flew over our positions and waved at us with their wings, rolling their planes from side to side. Hundreds of Kurds and other soldiers cheered them, hailing them with outstretched arms. "Obama! Obama!" they shouted.

I could not get Kemal out of my mind. I found it hard to believe that he was dead. The Kurds had also been fond of Kemal, and the mood around the fire this evening was solemn. Some of those who had known Kemal longer than me, wept. Kemal's death appalled and distressed me, but I did not cry. I don't believe that grief need be connected with death. Death is a natural and essential part of life, especially for a soldier. As such it should be celebrated. Our sorrow is selfish and culturally determined. Man actually grieves for his own loss, not for the dead. The dead feel no pain and they wouldn't like to see their beloved grieve and be miserable.

Indeed, many cultures around the world consider death a natural and important aspect of life. There we see no tears. In the West, however, we are expected to cry or show our remorse. But the truth is that, instead of going through all the stages of denial, anger, frustration, depression, and acceptance associated with the loss of someone you love, you may as well jump straight to the last stage, which is acceptance, and appreciate that life without death does not have meaning. Of course, the situation is different when someone dies prematurely at a tender age.

But to be completely shattered by the loss is to no avail.

16. Attack

We had spent the night in a typical Arabic house of clay, with floors of soil, and holes in the walls as windows. The residents had apparently left in haste, for there were still many possessions left. There were photos of Arab men with scarf around their heads on the wall. There were never any pictures of women or children in the houses.

It often bothered me to sleep in abandoned settlements. I felt like an intruder. I tried to soothe my conscience by thinking that they would be able to return one day, when the Daesh would no longer be around to make their lives miserable.

All houses had virtually the same simple interior: tea sets, blankets and mattresses, pillows to sit and sleep on, limited kitchen-ware, a few shelves, and some plastic chairs. There was almost no furniture in the houses. I used to find a space in the room from which I could easily get out to the toilet at night without having to stumble over 10 other hevals. I made sure to place my blankets away from others' feet, as we seldom got to wash. As it was difficult to wash clothes, underwear was only changed about once a week.

The rooms always seemed to smell bad: like a stable with animals. Buddhist traditions had taught me that it was I who disturbed the smells and sounds, and that it was not the smells and sounds that disturbed me. It had taken me a long time to understand this strange reasoning, but it did eventually sink in. And it made it easier for me to accept this kind of discomfort. But I didn't see any point in looking for unpleasant odours, especially not the stink of unwashed soldiers' feet!

I was particularly bothered if I found toys in the houses. It made me think that it could have been my own daughter who had been forced to flee. It was something I couldn't bear to imagine, and quickly repressed these thoughts.

It was much the same routine every day. Get up early and light a fire to make tea, food, and to get warm by. We'd clean our weapons and equipment if we had been in action. The Russian weapons are built with relatively large mechanical tolerances, and therefore rarely malfunction. They didn't really need to be cleaned so often, which is perfect for war in a very dusty environment. However, as gunpowder residues influence precision, I cleaned my barrel with a pull-through every time I had fired it.

The days passed quickly with these daily chores. The sun began to set in the western horizon and threw its customary reddish warm glow over Rojave.

We expected to attack a Daesh position which was only a few minutes' drive to the south. We prepared ourselves to move in shortly after the bombs had been dropped, while the Daesh were still shaken by attacks from our angels in the air.

We boarded the vehicles and headed towards the enemy. We positioned our vehicles strategically so that we had optimal shooting opportunities against the Daesh. At the same time, we made sure to keep so much distance between the vehicles that the enemy would have to move their weapons to target us. This would make it more difficult to concentrate their fire on us.

The roar of jet engines and drones with propellers hang constantly in the sky above us, to the extent that, rather than noticing the sound itself, we only noticed it when it sometimes stopped. Suddenly there was a loud whistle and a boom in the air above our heads, followed by a huge explosion. Everyone cheered out loudly when the bomb exploded in a plume of smoke and flames. The Kurds shouted: "Obama! Obama! ". It wasn't necessarily the US President's aircraft that dropped the bombs, although it was likely. It could've been planes from any number of countries from the now large coalition that was fighting IS.

Another five or six violent explosions went off within the next 10 to 15 minutes There was then a pause in the attacks. We got ourselves ready to go on the offensive. I told the hevals with me that the time had now come for the Daesh to pay for Kemal's death. I could see their eyes tightened in anger and determination, inspiring them with an even more fervent fighting spirit.

When we started driving towards the Daesh position we all shouted: "For Kemal!"

The engine of our second Humvee had blown a gasket, so Soran and I had now manned a Russian APC (armoured personnel carrier) instead. He had asked me to man the tower where Kemal had been when he'd been killed the day before. I was therefore seated up front with the heavy Dushka-machine gun. Shingal, a young veteran from Shingal, was in the hatch in the middle of our personnel carrier, armed with a Bisfink rocket launcher (RPG).

We had filled the vehicle with crates of ammunition for the Kalash, PKC, and the Bisfink rocket launcher. It was cramped inside, but at least we were protected by the steel of the vehicle against light weapons.

The many Dushka machine guns from the different vehicles simultaneously opened fire at the Daesh positions inside the town. Like red lasers in the sky, the dark and now chilly night was criss-crossed with countless explosions and red tracer bullets. It was slightly reminiscent of a scene from Star Wars. The firing came from many positions in a wide arc around the city. It was a fantastic spectacle. The moon was nearly full and threw its pale light over the town and fields. I was glad of this, as it was hard to manoeuvre in the dark of the night.

Inside the armoured vehicle, the old diesel engine roared. It smelled of warm lubricating oil, diesel and rubber.

We were approaching the village from where we could be fired upon at any moment from the Daesh's positions. We kept our heads down and only looked over the edges of the vehicles hatches. The red tracer bullets from our own ranks began to be fired eerily close to us. I shouted to Soran that we should beware of "friendly fire".

At the same time some uneasy thoughts became lodged in my head: Did all the machine gunners make radio contact? Had all our gunners remembered to charge their batteries so we could prevent any "friendly fire"? Did everybody know that we had now driven into the town? Or would they shoot at everything and everyone in the town, including us? I had to dismiss these worries and focus on the Daesh! Still, the thought of being shot at by our own heavy weapons and guns was pretty scary. I knew that our APC couldn't protect us from that kind of fire, especially from the rear, where our armour was thinnest.

We first drove towards the eastern part of the town, where the Daesh had already started shooting at us. Once again, bullets whistled above our heads: a sound that had now become so familiar that it didn't bother me much. It was RPG rockets I was most afraid of.

With all the other noise around, I tried to filter out the sound of rockets, with their high whistling signature sound. Suddenly I heard this very whistle … SSSHHHsss ! I saw a RPG rocket, but it flew in a different direction. But the very sight and sound of the rocket was enough to give me heart palpitations. A good RPG operator could fire one rocket after another in quick succession, especially if he had a charger to assist him.

We returned fire, but it was not easy to aim with any precision while the armoured vehicle was in motion.

The driver had to keep the APC on the move to make it as difficult as possible for the Daesh to hit us.

At the same time, our infantry was advancing towards the town from the north and east. They ran from cover to cover – and through cover – whenever possible. It was a simple but vital tactic during any advance. As I knew that everybody listened to Soran, I had discussed it with him. Sure enough, they had begun to put this tactic into practice; at least to a greater extent than I had experienced during previous skirmishes.

There was suddenly a huge blast. I suspected that a mine had been detonated. But in the dark I couldn't see what had triggered it. Suddenly, communications went back and forth over the radio. I could hardly understand a word being shouted through our hand transmitters. I did, however, recognise a few words. Most of all, they shouted, "*Leda!*" (fire).

We then received an order over the radio. The driver first turned towards the north and then to the west, until we headed into the western side of the village. There were some small houses there from which shots were fired. I was about to return fire. But although it appeared as though the shots had been fired at us, I hadn't noticed the familiar sound of whistling bullets above our heads. Nor was there any noise of bullets banging against our vehicle.

I held fire until I was sure that it was not our own troops. This was fortunate, because soon afterwards

Soran told me that there were now friendlies (own troops) in some of those buildings. We had to be very careful what we shot at. I was extremely uncomfortable in this situation, when our own troops were so close to the Daesh's positions.

The darkness didn't make it any easier to distinguish our own men from the enemy. I was aware of the limited experience that our forces had in this kind of night battle, in the dark, with many vehicles. And, on top of that, in a built-up area. I started to think that it had been a mistake to launch us into this kind of battle under these circumstances. There was too much room for error, with enormous consequences. If you happened to kill one of your own comrades by accident, it is by no means certain that you'd ever get over it. Your morale would certainly wane, and you probably wouldn't be able to find the will to fight on. But now I was in the middle of it. I had to rid my head of these thoughts, and do my best.

I noticed that one of our machine guns was firing at a building, and that fire was being returned from this building. My Dushka in the tower had, meanwhile, been malfunctioning. I pulled up my PKC from the bottom of the vehicle. I found a resting place for it on the edge of the tower and began firing at the building from which I could see muzzle fire.

But suddenly the PKC also had a malfunction, which it rarely had: not least because I kept it so clean, and because all its parts were in good working order. I looked around, and discovered that the ammunition belt had jammed in something that stuck out of the tower. I swore loudly.

The tower didn't work properly. When the vehicle was going down a slope, the tower swung around madly. It was obviously some stupid mechanic, who had had the brilliant idea of mounting two metal arms for extra protection, but too far out from the tower. Their weight and momentum swung the tower wildly whenever the vehicle was at an angle on a slope. This mechanic had clearly not considered that an armoured vehicle is not always driving on flat ground.

Rather than the tower swinging around wildly every time we moved down a slope, they could easily have made a bolt that locked the tower in a fixed position.

I managed to loosen the ammunition belt and continued firing. But every time the vehicle turned, I had to move the PKC to make sure that the ammo belt pulled unhindered through the machine gun when I fired. It was hard work, which made me sweat profusely. The PKC alone weighed 8 kg. But with several hundred rounds as well, it easily weighed 13 kg. On top of this, the position where I lifted it was too high up. Occasionally I burnt my hands on the now blistering hot barrel. I could not put on gloves. I needed the sensitivity of my fingers to reload and loosen the ammo belt from time to time. So I swallowed the pain, which was relatively easy. When you're under fire, even severe pain is not felt in the same way.

We headed towards a small bridge, which was the only access to the town. The Daesh had used excavators to build a rampart around the entire settlement. We stopped beside the bridge. I noticed some people lying in a ditch next to it. I was astonished to suddenly see them so close to the vehicle. With the enemy so close up, I grabbed my Kalash, which was quicker and easier to handle than a PKC. To my relief, I recognized the uniforms and bandanas typically worn by the Kurdish militia.

From now on, I would concentrate on not only shooting at the enemy, but also being vigilant about soldiers approaching our vehicle from any direction. The Daesh often used suicide tactics, and a Daesh could easily attack us from the side or from behind. If they succeeded in throwing a grenade into our vehicle – that would be the end of us.

I couldn't see clearly what they were doing in the ditch, but there were several people down there. As I could hear groaning from the depth of the ditch, I assumed that there were several injured, and that the vehicle would now be used for its secondary purpose, as an ambulance on the front lines. Sure enough, wounded hevals were brought in through the hatches on the back of the vehicle.

The driver revved up, and we sped off in an easterly direction towards our advanced base. The driver raced and swerved, as much to avoid buildings and electricity poles as to avoid enemy fire. Being built mostly of metal, riding inside an armoured vehicle is hardly a joyride. Unless you hold on tight, it is easy to end up being buckled and bruised.

Suddenly I heard the sound of a rocket ... "SSSHHHsss". A RPG flew close past our armoured vehicle. Too close. Shingal had seen where the rocket had come from, and returned fire with our own RPG. There was a massive explosion as the rocket, which Shingal had fired, hit the building behind us. Whenever Shingal fired an RPG, it left behind a huge cloud of rocket smoke and a foul smell. You could taste the chemicals from the RPG in your mouth. If you were to stand less than a few metres behind the rocket when it was fired, you would be killed on the spot.

17. Back to the Present

I woke up from my day-dreams, which had started with the phone call from Yana last year. I was back in the house next to the dead Daesh with the smelly feet. I don't know how long I'd been lost in thought. But I was now back in the war. I had to clear my mind and focus.

We took turns taking guard at the window and returning fire on the Daesh position. We had two wounded hevals in the room, who occasionally groaned in pain. The erratically rush of pain searing through my back mad me swear out loud.

Suddenly we heard a crash just outside the building. We looked anxiously at one another. The other armoured vehicle had arrived to pull us out and had been shot at. But the driver had got unnerved, and had bumped into our vehicle with a thud. While he backed up, the crew had to get out and attach a steel cable to our vehicle. Not exactly a dream job under enemy fire.

We intensified our covering fire at the Daesh while they worked. They quickly attached the steel cable and began to pull our armoured vehicle out of the sand pit. It came out and drove to our entrance. We all got ready to jump back on board. This time we had the building for cover as we got into the vehicle. When we were all inside, we made our way back to our advanced base. The diesel engine revved up, and we sped off in a north-easterly direction.

Suddenly a heval shouted, "Stop!" I didn't understand everything he said, but the message was quite clear: we were short of a heval. Damn it! We had to go back again, which was the last thing we wanted to do right now.

The armoured vehicle turned around and we headed back. There was the heval on the corner of the building, looking desperately unhappy. We opened the door for him and he jumped in. He had been busy firing at the Daesh from another room and hadn't noticed that we'd left. It must have been an awful surprise to suddenly realise that he was alone in a fire-fight with the Daesh!

Rosa sat close up to me. I noticed that she was shaking; her big eyes staring into space. I offered her my jacket, but she refused. She had her own thick jacket. She was not cold. So instead I put my arm around her shoulder and hummed a Kurdish tune.

We made our way back to our advanced base and helped the wounded out. We were all exhausted after long hours of battle. Most of us had survived to fight another day.

But on this night, sitting around the fire, three heval in our tabur were missing.

I didn't catch much sleep that night. It was continually interrupted by firing and explosions, and a young Kurd lying close to me couldn't stop weeping. The three heval who had died were his "brothers". He was devastated. He tried to hide his tears, but didn't succeed. Sometimes he took a short break, but would then start weeping again. He didn't get out of bed for the next three days. Every time I came into the hut, I could feel his pain.

I was very worried about him. He was only 17 or 18 years old and should never have had to experience this kind of thing at such a young age. Had he been born in another country, he would undoubtedly have been busy playing football with his mates, chasing girls, or studying. He was distraught, but it wouldn't be long before he'd have to pull himself together and join in the fighting again; regardless of whether he was afraid of being killed or maimed.

We fought many days more before the Daesh abandoned the town and fled south and west.

IS troops had been weakened by our offensive. The Kurds were skilled strategists and had decades of experience in warfare. They wouldn't give the Daesh any opportunity to escape after the next attack, give them a chance to rest, get supplies, or regroup; because we would then just have to fight against those same soldiers again at a later date.

The Kurdish officers had therefore hatched a plan, to capture and destroy as many of the enemy as possible, when we next attacked a Daesh position. The plan was simple. When we advanced on a town, we would first move our flanks further past the town before we launched the attack.

The Kurdish troops on the flanks would then prevent the Daesh from escaping, as they had done during several previous offensives.

Our tabur was part of the northern flank tasked with intercepting the Daesh during their withdrawal. We had moved a few kilometres past the village where the Daesh had entrenched themselves in the district of southern Rojave, not far from Iraq.

Our other flank was only a few kilometres south of us and we were preparing a pincer manoeuvre. But we had to be careful and avoid getting too close to each other, as this risked friendly fire. By the same token, we couldn't let the Daesh's escape route be too broad and allow them to get through the corridor.

I had wondered why we didn't just surround the town completely. But Kurds were shrewd. Daesh scouts would notice that they were being encircled. They would then just remain in the city and fight fiercely to the last man, with huge losses for us and a waste of precious time.

Instead, it was far easier and quicker to harry the Daesh while they were on the run. And for this, it was necessary to give IS an escape route; or at least the illusion of having one.

Our tabur began to survey the terrain. We discussed which route the Daesh would most likely choose to escape from the city. The Daesh were not stupid. They would try to exploit the terrain as best they could. A wide ravine would seem to give them the best protection during a withdrawal.

We became reasonably confident that they would try to escape through this route. We therefore began to prepare the ravine with Claymore mines, which the Kurds had recently received, probably from the autonomous Kurdish region. I was familiar with Claymore mines, which were originally developed by the Germans during World War II. But I had never used them.

It rained for a change. But we didn't have time to wait for better weather, so we started placing the mines in the rain.

There were many well-trained soldiers in my tabur. A few knew about setting up explosives.

Together we planted the mines at intervals that would produce the most devastating effect.

We had eight mines, which was plenty. As soon as the Daesh triggered the first mines, the rest of their troops would try to find alternative escape routes, and we therefore wouldn't need more anti-personnel mines.

It was important that the mines were placed at the front of the ravine, and that as many as possible were triggered at the right time. We therefore placed mines that could be detonated manually (by pulling a trigger wire) in front at the entrance to the ravine. Around 30 metres into the ravine we placed our rear mines, which would be detonated by trip wires.

This would enable us to trap and destroy as many enemy soldiers as possible with mines before the rest of the Daesh fled along alternative escape routes.

We placed the mines along the sides of the ravine in a V-shaped pattern. As darkness fell, we hid the mines with small shrubs, and put a layer of soil over the wires.

Fortunately, the rain helped hide our tracks. Nevertheless, we agreed to return when it was light to ensure that we hadn't left behind traces during the dark that we had overlooked, and that could give away our ambush to the Daesh.

We turned our mines at a 45 degree angle facing forward, so that they would spread their deadly blast both sideways and backwards, and thus injure as many as possible.

It can be advantageous to injure your enemy rather than killing him. Injuring one's enemy would take several men out of the action at the same time, because it takes another two men to carry the wounded away. Furthermore, a screaming fellow soldier demoralises the other soldiers psychologically. If the wounded have to be transported to a hospital, this is a burden for the enemy's infrastructure and resources far down the chain. On the other hand, if an enemy is killed, his fellow soldiers can simply leave him or bury him.

With our mission complete, we drove back to our makeshift base.

The next morning we returned with our entire tabur. We inspected the ravine for signs of our presence, and Soran gave instructions to everyone, giving them their positions and telling them exactly what they had to do during the ambush.

In the meantime, we had received three new replacements for the heval we had lost during the last attack. It was two men and a woman, all in their early twenties. They had received military training, but had not fought at the very front before.

Soran made sure to place them so that they covered our back, in a position that was less dangerous.

Soran had by now several years of combat experience and was an excellent leader. I was proud to fight alongside him. The respect seemed mutual. Since the first time we had met, when he had picked me up in his Hummer, we had fought alongside each other in several battles.

The bond you develop when you are fellow survivors and when your lives depend on each other, are special. I had friends at home who I had known for years, but I doubted I knew them as well as I knew Soran, despite the fact that we had only been together for a few months.

Both Soran and I worried about whether our strategy was safe enough, and if we had thought everything through properly. We were both anxious about what could happen if the Daesh chose another escape route, or fled in several directions, or attacked us from behind.

We had to tighten up and make sure that our entire chain of troops covered each other's flanks all the way back to the village.

We therefore met with the other tabur. That all tabur were given a chance to voice their opinion was an advantage. It made it possible to consider several options, rather than just one commander's one-sided point of view. At least as long as there was sufficient time to discuss tactics, this democratic method of warfare strategy had many advantages. But we all knew that, in the heat of battle, it was Soran and the other commanders who gave the orders. There would then not be room for democratic niceties.

In this way, the Kurds got the best of both worlds. I was convinced that this approach was one of the reasons why we were so effective in battle.

We were getting busy. Our FAC (Forward Air Controller) had already called in air support for the attack on the town, and soon our armoured vehicles would go on the offensive.

It probably wouldn't take long before the first Daesh would begin to flee in our direction. We didn't know exactly how many troops the Daesh had in this area, but suspected that they had at least one company (150 men).

The wind had started blowing and, here in the southern part of Rojave, the landscape was very barren and sandy. It was therefore easy to get sand in your eyes, so I had started using my combat glasses, which looked a bit like ski goggles.

The whole time drones and fighter planes flew in the skies above us. They were mostly F18 aircrafts, probably from aircraft carriers in the Mediterranean. But there were also some F16 fighters that could not land on aircraft carriers. Therefore, they probably took off from Kuwait, or the British air base in Cyprus.

Turkey supported the Daesh, and had refused coalition aircrafts the use of their bases, despite the fact that Turkey was a member of NATO.

It was no secret that the Turkish government couldn't wait seeing the Syrian President Assad disposed, because they had a long and troubled history with the Assad regime.

But meanwhile, IS were fighting against the Kurds, who are the Turkish President Erdogan's arch enemy. Turkey therefore didn't treat the fight against the Daesh with any sense of urgency.

As was customary before an attack, several aircraft began circling in the airspace above the battle zone, and we knew that bombing would commence shortly.

We always welcomed this. Sure enough, not long afterwards there was an explosion in the town two kilometres behind us, sending up a column of smoke. Several more explosions followed in quick succession.

We had to prepare ourselves as there were always some Daesh who fled in panic when the first bombs fell.

When Soran gave us the order, we took up our assigned positions around the ravine. The two heval who were to trigger the Claymore mines were now down in the ravine behind some rocks.

I lay next to Soran behind some boulders which I had found and we used for cover. On the other side of Soran was Shingal with his RPG. And next to him was the young Kurd who helped Shingal load the rocket launcher.

Shortly after the first bomb had been dropped by a coalition aircraft, one of the Daesh's vehicles came driving over the fields at full speed. But the car went south of the ravine. We didn't shoot at it, partly because the vehicle was almost out of range, but also not to give away our position.

We could hear occasional shots being fired from our southern flank, but the vehicle sped on with a cloud of dust behind it.

Soon afterwards came another vehicle; this time a small truck. It also drove south of the ravine. We began to worry that we had misjudged the situation, and perhaps the Daesh would not use the ravine as an escape route after all.

But we continued to wait patiently. There were always some Daesh who fled on foot. There was still a high probability that they would use the large ravine. It was visible from a long distance and it stood out against the flat fields which offered no protection whatsoever.

By now, our armoured battalion had launched their attack. We could both see and hear the heavy fighting in the town, about two kilometres south-east of our position. We also followed the battle over the radio.

After a few hours came the announcement we had been waiting for. Several enemy soldiers had abandoned the town and had fled east on foot.

We tried to get their exact number, but the captain who provided the information was not sure about the enemy's size. He guessed that there were about 30 of them. What weapons they had, he could not see from a distance, not least because it was beginning to get dark.

But soon afterwards we heard the two other tabur that were covering our flank to the east, open fire. We couldn't see what was happening, but it sounded like heavy fighting.

Two enemy soldiers then came running directly towards the ravine. I looked at Soran. I could see that he had hoped for a larger number of soldiers. We didn't want to waste our mines on only two men. We were after "bigger fish"!

Instead, Soran called two marksmen armed with Karnas (Dragunov). I didn't understand what was being said, but I assumed that Soran had ordered them to take out the two fugitive Daesh.

As expected, the snipers lay down in position and got the escapees in their sights. The two Daesh were only about 200 metres away when they opened fire. The first shot didn't hit them, but the two Daesh stopped abruptly when they heard the shot, looked in our direction, and immediately threw themselves to the ground.

They shouldn't have done that. The next shot hit one of the Daesh. Through my binoculars, it looked as though he'd been hit in the head. Shortly afterwards, our next shot hit the second Daesh.

Soran ordered four heval into the opening of the ravine to remove the bodies. Soran didn't want to risk the other Daesh discovering them, and deciding to take an alternate escape route.

Soon afterwards, a Daesh vehicle approached at full speed from the town. They tried to break through our northern flank about 500 metres to the east of us.

At first, the tabur that was covering this part of our flank didn't manage to stop the vehicle. The Toyota with the Daesh soldiers had broken through. It was only stopped when one of our heval, who manned a heavy Dushka on the back of a Toyota pickup, opened fire.

There were about 10 Daesh. They were heavily armed and offered strong resistance. They managed to fire an RPG at our Toyota that had stopped them. The rocket struck our Toyota with a huge blast.

The rocket killed the heval who had operated the Dushka and the driver. I felt that Soran was both furious and worried. With the exception of Shingal and me, he ordered the rest of our tabur to remain in their positions.

The three of us ran together towards the vehicle with the Daesh. As we got closer, we were attacked with machine-gun fire, and had to dive for cover. A few metres to the right of us were the two dead heval, and one who had been injured. One of the dead I could not recognize, as his head had been partly blown off. But I recognised the second. It was the young heval that had been so devastated by the loss of his three brothers a few days earlier.

I couldn't take my eyes off him. He lay open-mouthed, staring blankly skyward. I was overwhelmed by a mixture of sadness and anger, and I felt a tear running down my cheek. I really wanted to cry, but I had to turn my grief into anger, otherwise I wouldn't be able to focus on fighting and surviving.

I crawled on all fours up to him, put my hand over his face, and closed his eyes. My thoughts were soon interrupted, for the third heval, only about 18 years old, had been shot in the chest and had difficulty breathing. He wept and spoke in Kurdish and from time to time screamed in agony. His hands and body were covered with blood. I tore his thin camouflage shirt open, and soon found the bullet hole in his left chest. A quiet stream of blood pulsated out of the hole and ran down his pale skin.

Shingal had joined us now. Meanwhile, Soran laid down heavy fire at the Daesh with my Pixie. This was good, as it made the Daesh cover themselves, and thus prevent them from aiming at us properly.

The other tabur was also firing at the vehicle with the Daesh.

It appeared that most Daesh had been killed or wounded by now.

Shingal turned the young heval over on his stomach to find the spot where the bullet had come out of his back. We did not have to search, because there was a large hole the size of an orange where the bullet had gone through. There was a pool of blood on the grass field. Shingal and I looked at each other without saying anything. We both thought the same thing.

Shingal stroked his hair, like a parent who soothes his small child, as he spoke softly to him. I did not understand the words, but from the tone of voice I knew what he said. Every person who has had the love of parents understands this universal language of love.

The young heval body went limp a few seconds later, as he lost consciousness and died.

Shingal stared vacantly into the air. I sensed he had gotten used to losing mates and had no more tears.

An RPG finished off the last two Daesh. We met with the other Tabur briefly to assess the situation. But we had little time so we hurried back to our tabur.

The funerals of our comrades had to wait until after the fighting was over. More Daesh could come at any moment, and we had to maintain our readiness.

But no more Daesh came during the next few hours, so we got ourselves prepared for a long cold night on the ground near the ravine.

I woke up when a heval shook me hard. "They're coming," he said in English. I was immediately wide awake, albeit a bit dazed.

It was still night, and in the background you could see the lights of the burning houses in the town. The grass around me was damp with dew, and it smelled of wet earth and gun-fire from Pixie beside me.

I had no idea for how long I had dozed off. Although my heart beat quickened at the thought of the Daesh being nearby, I had got used to fighting. I yawned while I made sure that Pixie was ready for action.

The many burning houses in the town threw long silhouettes of the Daesh moving towards the ravine.

I saw Soran crawling back and forth, making sure that everyone in our tabur was ready for action. We had distributed extra grenades and ammunition to those who only had a little left.

I had recently been provided with new German grenades after I had killed several Daesh with the old pineapple ones.

The general rule amongst the Kurds was that the further towards the front you fought, and the more enemies you killed, the better equipment you were issued. As our tabur was now one of the most effective, and with most battle experience, we all had relatively new equipment.

I counted the number of Daesh … 4, 7, 12, 13 men… that was about how many they were. They did not move tactically, and they must have felt relatively safe cause they spoke in Arabic, loud enough that we could hear them.

Two of the Daesh walked a little ahead and were now only a few metres from our first manually operated Claymore mine.

I lay still trying to avoid making the slightest sound. My heart was pounding faster as I took aim with Pixie at the largest group of Daesh.

I was sure that the mine would kill the ones in front, so I decided to concentrate Pixie's fire at the larger group for maximum effect.

The heval who operated the mines let the first two Daesh walk past the front mines, as agreed. The third mine was connected to a tripwire, which would trigger in a few seconds.

I wondered how big the explosion would be. I had never seen a Claymore detonate, but knew they could do serious damage.

The two Daesh were now right where the first tripwire had been strung out, and I prepared myself for the detonation. But to my surprise, they both walked on. Whether they had stepped over the trip wire, or whether there was a fault, it wasn't possible to know now. But a few seconds later, they stepped into the tripwire of the second mine, triggering a massive explosion.

Both Daesh were blasted to the side, and flew several metres through the air. But to my surprise, one Daesh stood up again. He was in shock, moving around in circles. He seemed to be looking for something on the ground. He bent down and picked up his arm, which had been blown off. A few seconds later he fell down on his knees, bent forward, and hit his head on the ground.

We all opened fire on the other Daesh. They ran away from us towards the southern opening of the ravine, hoping to find cover. This they would soon regret.

At that same moment, our two heval clicked the remote controls that triggered the front mines, killing and wounding four or five Daesh. Another three of four Daesh lay wounded or dead on the ground.

But there were still three Daesh who had managed to find cover behind a rock. Shingal ran closer and began throwing grenades at them. After the second grenade blew up, a wounded Daesh came out in sight with his weapon in outstretched arms.

Two heval ran towards him and ordered him down on his knees. As they got nearer, they approached him carefully with their Kalash pointed at him.

The Daesh soldier had large bulging eyes and a tormented look. He was bleeding from one ear and quietly reciting a prayer from the Koran.

Unfortunately, the two heval didn't notice this in the dark at first. Nor did they notice that he was holding a hand grenade partially hidden in one hand. They approached the Daesh carefully keeping him in the rifle sights. The two heval were not the most experienced, although they had fought several battles. Had they been at the front longer they would have known better than to approach a Daesh in such fashion.

The pin had already been pulled out, when one heval finally realised that the Daesh was praying. He screamed, "Cover!" while running away from the Daesh. But it was too late. The Daesh detonated the grenade by letting go its handle, sending shrapnel flying in all directions. One heval was killed immediately when the shrapnel struck his head and neck. The other heval survived: only just. However, he would never be able to fight again.

Soran was furious and bitter about another needless loss of life. He walked over to the dead Daesh, and cursed as he kicked the lifeless body in the side. I believe Soran wished he could revive the dead Daesh so that he could kill him one more time!

18. The River

We had liberated yet another village. But none of us felt much joy. The Daesh had had more losses than us, but we had lost too many hevals to feel that we had anything to celebrate.

Although we were victorious, the capture of a piece of land or a village cannot compensate for the loss of dead friends, and our victories seem to come at an increasingly high price.

Some heval who had fought from the beginning of the war, had lost all their friends and didn't recognize their own tabur anymore, since it had been completely replaced by new troops.

We continued the campaign in the west. Over the coming weeks and months, we besieged one town after another. If the Daesh offered stiff resistance, we called in the planes, and then moved into the town.

I gradually began to feel tired. We didn't sleep much anymore. When we finally did fall asleep, we would often be awoken by shots or bombs. I had lost a lot of weight by now. My body was covered with wounds and bruises. On my hands I had big burn blisters from Pixie's hot barrel. I began to long to get away from the war. I could feel that I was more tense and that my patience was running thin. I got irritated over small things, which in the past had not bothered me much. War, violence and the hard life at the front was beginning to wear me down both physically and mentally.

I had now been away from home for five months totally and I knew that there were limits to what my wife and my child could stand. Although I had not told her that I was fighting at the front of the front line, she was understandably still very worried about me. I also thought a lot about my daughter and how she would react, and how her life would be affected if I were to perish at war. My mailbox was undoubtedly overflowing with window envelopes and bills. I had to start thinking about getting north and sorting out my private affairs. I was due a few weeks of leave by now, anyway. I could always come back later.

During an attack, one of our foreign soldiers had fled the battle field in panic. I could certainly understand why Dan (not his real name) had done so. But it had left the rest of us vulnerable. I had a chat with him. Although he himself believed that he had not yet finished his job in Syria, I told him that he had, not least because he also seemed mentally unstable. I offered to accompany Dan back to headquarters, as I was going there anyway. I requested a vehicle and explained the situation to the driver. We had not gone very far when Dan flung open the door while we were doing 30 or 40 km/h, and jumped out the car. He rolled over and ran off at a sprint towards the nearest village. The driver and I looked at each other aghast. We turned around and drove slowly after Dan. We let him exhaust himself running in front of the car. When he came to the village where a company stayed, he started to look for something in the buildings. Shortly afterwards, he came out of one of the houses with a bag of nuts in his hand. He came up to us to explain that he had forgotten his food. It only confirmed that he was ripe for repatriation and treatment.

We drove off once more, heading for HQ, and Dan behaved fairly normally during the rest of the trip.

There was no problem about being granted leave. The management at the headquarters had been particularly pleased with our effort. At the headquarters there was a foreign soldier who I had known for a while. He was also going east. We agreed to travel back together across the river to Iraq. At times there could be a long wait to get over the River Tigris. Peshmerga had increased their vigilance after being pressured by the coalition. We had heard about soldiers who had waited a full 14 days to cross the border. We didn't have the time to wait that long.

I passed through the Academy to say goodbye to Renas and the other instructors. In the meantime, yet more foreigners had arrived at the Academy, and the school was full up. The new recruits were standing outside smoking in the sun when I arrived. I found Renas and we had lunch together. Afterwards I gave him my knife as a thank you for his hospitality. I could sense that he was touched. He went into his office and came out with his prayer beads in his hands. Renas handed me the beads. I did appreciate his gesture, not least because they are such a very personal possession. We kissed each other on the cheek and said goodbye.

Two days later we received a message telling us to get ready for departure.

We left the headquarters in haste under cover of darkness, and the driver sped down the mountain. I had the feeling that the window of opportunity that had opened, could quickly close again. Now it became urgent to cross the border as soon as possible, while we still could. We arrived at a border crossing, but a guerrilla came to tell us that we couldn't make the crossing using this route.

We then headed south down a small dirt road. At the end of the dirt track the driver switched off the lights and we drove for a while without them. In the background, we could now make out the Tigris. The river glinted from the spotlights that shone on it from the Iraqi side. The driver stopped the car. We got out and continued on foot along a narrow path that ran down along the river.

After about a half-hour's march we came to where an inflatable boat that had been hidden behind some large rocks and logs. We started to pump it up. In addition to the foreign soldier and myself, there was also the guide and another five Kurds in our group. The Kurds were armed with M16 rifles and night vision binoculars. They kept watch while we pumped up the dinghy. When the boat had been inflated, we carried it down to the river. The guide cautioned us to be completely quiet.

On the opposite bank there was an excavator busy reinforcing the border. It pushed up soil into steep embankments all the way to the river. After about an hour of waiting, the excavator drove off. We put the dinghy in the water and got in. The armed Kurds lay on the side of the dinghy with their weapons and night vision binoculars. They looked like frogmen on a commando mission.

In the distance we could see a cigarette glow from a Peshmerga border guard. It was chilly and his breath and smoke made a large cloud when he exhaled.

The stars were shining from a clear bright sky. Tigris was very quiet this night, most animals were sleeping and there was no wind. A mist hung above the river and had it not been for the dangerous situation, I would have enjoyed this peaceful river crossing.

We let the current take us while we slowly paddled toward the opposite side. We all kept completely silent as we approached the river bank. A guerrilla was waiting to receive us. While we went ashore, another group of soldiers moved down towards the boat. We shook hands as we walked past each other. These guerrillas were heading in the opposite direction, to the war in Syria.

As we walked through a field, our trousers got wet from dew on the grass. When we arrived at the other end of the field, we had to cross a road. But as there was the occasional car coming, we had to jump for cover each time to avoid being caught in the car-lights. We made our way over a bumpy field and climbed up a steep hill. After another hour's march, we arrived at a dirt road, where a vehicle was waiting. It would take us to a guerrilla camp not far away in a ravine by a small mountain. After arriving at the camp, we were given a cup of tea and then went to bed.

The next day we got up early, both the other soldier and I had to move on quickly to Erbil.

The rest of the trip to Erbil went uneventfully. But upon arrival at Erbil we were stopped at a checkpoint.

I had to call Captain Kameran from Asayish to enable us to proceed. Meanwhile, we showed the police our photos from the war.

They were amazed that we had travelled so far and had risked our lives to help the Kurds. They were not accustomed to the outside world caring much about their problems. They gave us a hug and kisses on our cheeks and called us brothers.

The war and the experiences in Syria will forever be a part of me.

The Kurds taught me a lot about respect, patience, hospitality, and not least courage. I will always remember the men and women whom I fought with in Syria and Kurdistan. "You shall not pass!" was their rallying cry to the Islamic State.

These brave people, some of them no more than big kids, have only few of the riches that most of us value so much. In our part of the world wealth and fame make idols. But there on the battlefields of Syria fight, in my eyes, the true kings and queens.

Petite Rosa, only 18 years old, with her big machine gun, is trying to liberate her country from a terrible enemy. She does not want this war, but her family lives in Al Qamishlo, not far from the front, and she has no choice but to fight. A small girl with a heart whose size it is difficult to grasp. As long as Rosa and the other heval sacrifice their lives at the front, many others can live.

Sometimes when I dream, I am back on the River Tigris. The sun is shining and a wonderful fresh, cooling breeze dances on the sparkling water. There are so many beautiful birds and flowering trees right here along its river banks. I try to capture them in my mind and push away the darkness. If I look too far down the river, I will quickly drift past, and catch only a fleeting glimpse of this paradise. And if I turn around and look back, I will see the ghosts of the past, and might even drown.

    I cannot swim against the floodwaters, and I must accept that the Tigris leads me where it wants. I put my hands behind my head and lean back while I slowly glide away. I smell the scent of jasmine and spring onions, and the sun's rays shine on my dusty face through the treetops.